Happy Tails

2-

"An insightful self-help book that will be a boon to anyone seeking to end a difficult relationship and reclaim their happiness."

—David Borcherding

Former editor, Writer's Digest Books

"Julie Rogers has written a beautiful book of stories about her feelings as she faced her dilemma of a marriage break-up. Each demon was tamed by an animal that became her teacher . . . imaginatively, she projected her dilemmas onto pets she cared for or came across in distress. She was looking for learning in all the right places, serendipitously finding plenty in each. By turning her own anguish into compassionate connections with the simplicity and innocence of her animal friends, she found her own inner wisdom and healing.

Happy Tails *will be a comforting and spiritually uplifting book for those struggling with the ending of a relationship and searching for emerging inner strength and newness in identity."*

— Dwight Webb, Ph.D., Psychologist

University of New Hampshire

Author of *Fifty Ways to Love Your Leaver: Getting on With Your Life After the Breakup*

www.impactpublishers.com

Happy Tails

How Pets Can Help You Survive Divorce

Julie Rogers

Happy Tails: How Pets Can Help You Survive Divorce

Printed and bound in the United States of America.

For information, please contact Brown Books, 16200 N. Dallas Parkway, Suite 225, Dallas, Texas 75248

ISBN 0-9706108-0-7
First Printing 2001

Brown Books
brownbooks.com

To my grandmother,
who taught me love has a will.

Contents

Part II—Intimacy

Foreword

Grieving a divorce differs from other losses. In this book, my friend Julie Rogers adds an original approach to this often written about subject. Most of us know that pets can help heal emotional wounds. We see them used in hospitals, rehabilitation centers, and nursing homes. This book takes us a step further. Julie takes the struggles and triumphs of injured and abandoned animals and relates them to our own. She takes the pain of abandonment as well as the pure, unconditional love of specific, exceptional pets and identifies these intense emotions with our own—in a way that shows how all living beings share the need for love.

This book is an honest examination of Julie's personal journey through the death of her first marriage and the ambivalence that inevitably accompanies the ending of a relationship. She covers all aspects of the breakup in a truly honest and vulnerable way, carrying the reader through to her own happy ending. Julie even owns up to her own part in the breakup, an exemplary undertaking for anyone experiencing a divorce. Through her experience, we see that by accepting certain responsibilities, we can understand and even have compassion for a former spouse, which is the key to healing.

Julie's emotional connection to animals shines through her writing and shows us that if we can step outside ourselves to care about other living beings, be it human or four-legged creatures, such love can carry us through anything.

—Lynn Courtney
Licensed Professional Counselor

Preface

Of the many people who assisted me in completing this book, I wish to pay special tribute to my friend, adventure novelist Michael Reisig. It's not a stretch to say that this book wouldn't have been published without his vision. As we neared our completion date at Brown Books publishing company—just weeks away from going to press—Michael lost a ten-year companion and friend, his Rottweiler, Ra.

Ra's name has its origins in the ancient Egyptian worship of the sun god Ra, a symbol of divinity and spiritual enlightenment. The sun, Egyptians believed, was God's closest earthly representative. As I came to see, Michael couldn't have chosen a more appropriate name for his dog.

Michael wears a salt-and-pepper beard, rolls up his sleeves, and straps on a Leatherman to work, usually with a ready twinkle in his eye. In his weekly newspaper column, *The Intrepid Arkansas Traveler,* Michael wrote often about his favorite and trusty fishing companion, Ra. A lover of the great outdoors and a seasoned survivalist, Michael writes a weekly column that covers everything from the best new spinner bait for angling on the Cossatot to the latest game and fishing laws. Ra was a huge part of the serenity and oneness with nature that Michael found while fishing the churning waters of the Ouachita River.

Knowing Ra was Michael's personal experience of, simply, *the remarkable.* Like the other animals in this book, Ra was a teacher, a friend, and a survivor. Michael rescued Ra from a new and confused mother who turned away her pups when Ra was barely three weeks old. He also experienced on that day the unique and indelible owner's honor of being chosen—by Ra, a bundle of fur and all legs that squirmed his way out of the pack and waggled over to meet Michael eye to eye.

Michael took Ra home and bottle-fed him around the clock.

I think I understood Michael's need to relive those happy moments when I visited with him one afternoon shortly after Ra's death. Michael was ill himself—he'd caught a bad summer cold from too many sleepless nights during his monthlong ordeal of caring for Ra. He began by telling me with a chuckle about Ra's first baby bark and a hearty, comic attempt to stand his ground inside a tiny wicker basket just hours after he'd settled into his new home.

Michael had talked often about Ra's gentleness with smaller creatures and his extraordinary refusal to prey upon weaker species. Although certainly formidable-looking at 140 pounds, Ra, he said, had a gentle nature and the personality of a curious child. Michael explained that while Rottweilers are often expected to be vicious, he'd raised Ra as a gentle companion, and Ra had rewarded his effort tenfold.

I wasn't convinced. "He refused to prey on anything at all?"

Michael smiled. "Oh, he loved to chase everything; he never caught anything. It wasn't for lack of ability. I think he figured if he started catching things, word would get around and no one would want to play anymore."

I agree with Michael that if we go the extra mile with loving attention to our pets, they will often repay our devotion by extending themselves beyond our firmest preconceptions, surpassing even the traits and limitations of their own breed.

The amazing capacity of animals to sense the conundrums of the human heart—to see the weight of the world on our shoulders and be there for us—is something Michael knew well with Ra.

Michael pulled pictures out of his desk drawer. They showed a massive and muscular black dog with chestnut markings on the legs and face. His eyes were bright and inquisitive. Ra was the largest Rottweiler I'd ever seen.

Michael picked out a photo of Ra lying by him in his front yard. "He could always tell if things weren't right with me," he said. "He would gently lay that huge head on my chest and look up at me with those dark, understanding eyes. I could almost hear him saying, 'I'm here. Need to talk?'"

"Ra loved to go fishing with me," he went on. "He'd explore along the water's edge, occasionally wading in to cool off, always wanting a close look at each fish I caught."

A dislocated hip complicated by kidney failure eventually took Ra from Michael, but not without a good, hard fight. Ra, he explained, had been very sick before—surviving even snakebites and other illnesses with a strong spirit. Michael expected Ra to fight, but when it became evident he was losing, Michael hugged his car's steering wheel every morning before work and tearfully prayed.

After several trips to the vet, repeated blood draws, and dutifully administered antibiotics and electrolytes, Ra's struggles to stand became more and more pronounced. Michael recalled for me his last night with his friend, before the decision to euthanize him the next day.

"The last night his lungs began to fill with fluid, and he couldn't lay his head down without choking and vomiting. I'd sat up with him for days, elevating his head, stroking him, telling him how much he meant to me. I remember laying my face against his neck that final night and inhaling that sweet, musty smell of his fur, hoping desperately that I might remember that smell for the rest of my life."

Ra continued to take an unpalatable electrolyte mixture without a fuss and never showed signs of surrender. He also made sure he gave Michael an appropriate number of reassuring nudges in those last hours.

"He would look at me with those tired, sad eyes, ease his head over, and touch me with his muzzle, as if to say, 'It's okay, my friend. It's okay.' " Michael described his decision to euthanize Ra as one of those stone-cold gray choices, the greatest paradox of them all, to love a creature enough to take its life. The next morning he was at the veterinarian's, kneeling by Ra while an anesthetic overdose was administered.

I heard peace in Michael's voice, but his trademark twinkle didn't reach his eyes.

"I watched the terrifying finality of it all and held Ra's head in my hands," he said. "I whispered words of hollow reassurance and love long after I knew he was gone."

Michael wrote a poignant farewell column about his dog just a few days after Ra died, an exquisitely painful exercise of generosity and, well, guts. In it, he told of many more defining moments—the footprints in the sand, man beside his best friend—that remain forever cast as his most special memories.

I include Michael's painful experience because, for me, his is the substance and summary of this book. It is a story of the grace animals offer us—love in its purest form, devoid of false colors—the only strings attached being our eternal enrichment.

Yes, I believe animals offer sacred moments. Though neither Michael nor I profess to know what happens to animals when they die, Michael admits he hopes to find Ra waiting for him on the other side, where they will fish the rivers in the sky, side by side again.

So do I.

Acknowledgments

Now that *Happy Tails* stands on its own, I have, of course, several people to acknowledge. First I'd like to thank my family: my father, mother, aunts, uncles, and cousins who were there when I needed you most. I love you all.

Next to my family are personal friends like Mary Lynn Baxter, Patsy and Wally Dunks, Lynn Courtney, Rebecca Flynt, and Michael Reisig who saw me through the process. Thanks, too, to Verla Huckaby, who had hope for the book at a very early reading.

In addition to friends is a whole load of clients in Lufkin, Texas who kept me busy working when I needed to be occupied. You kept me sane.

Thanks, too, to Bill and Agnes Rogers for your unwavering, keen interest and knowledge about writing in the raw.

Of course, *Happy Tails* would not exist as it does today without the indispensable touch of my editor, June Ford. Thanks for all the midnight e-mail.

Two readers who also devoted many hours to the copy are Rebecca Flynt and Claire O'Daniel. Hats off to you.

Thanks to Bill Pitchford, DVM, for your painstaking details about animals when I asked, and your absolute dedication to your calling. We need more like you.

And to those who took the time to give your two-cents on the package, particularly the cover: Dale Powell, Melanie Rigney, Rich Krevolin, Richard Cohn, Chris Vogler, and the gang at Brown Books: Milli, Suzanna, and Kathryn. Kudos and more kudos to you.

My many thanks, too, to Milli Brown for her unflinching first look at my offbeat vision and her willingness to guide it into reality.

Last and certainly not least, my deepest appreciation to the two men in my life who help make living a joyous experience—my husband, Jim, and our son.

Introduction

Dear Reader,

As you read, you may wonder (and rightfully so) if certain animals were chosen over others, or if the stories fall in certain sequence. The answers are yes and yes. The book is divided into nineteen chapters, and in it I include only animal stories that, to me, are parallel in theme with the stages of my divorce recovery. These stages are arranged in tandem, or how most people I've talked to experienced them. They are: separation, loneliness, denial, anger, bargaining, bottoming out, understanding, acceptance, setting goals, taking action, and forgiveness. No, you don't have to memorize them, and there won't be a pop quiz at the end. Keep in mind that these are only my buzzwords and my stories. You might like to come up with a few of your own—whatever works for you.

Here I must credit Dr. Elisabeth Kubler-Ross and Dr. Dwight Webb for their work in identifying the emotional patterns and hurdles most people encounter during grief experiences. Their research provides the blueprint for Part 1 of this book. Dr. Kubler-Ross started with five stages, which Dr. Webb insightfully doubled to ten. He explains in his book *Divorce & Separation Recovery* that the grief stages for getting past divorce are greater in number because the grief is more complex. I added one to the total: separation—a very significant step to me—though separating before divorce doesn't necessarily occur in everyone's experience.

I like to think of Part II as a special journey for establishing a new intimacy after such a devastating loss. In it are eight stages, eight stories—which parlay some personal alternatives and different companionship dynamics I encountered the second time around. They are: attraction, friendship, laying foundations, commitment, expectations, sharing good and bad, unity, and finally, appreciating the mastery of life. Again, I added a final stage to the original list—a bookend, or summary, which stands opposite the beginning—for those darkest hours when you may still ask yourself *why*.

Since it's always been easy for me to emotionally connect with animals (and many people I know share this experience), I chose their stories as a springboard to launch you, the reader, through the process. For, as I think you will see, the animals really are talking. All we need to do is listen.

Some of the best advice I got after my divorce (and I was feeling lower than sidewalk bug scum) came from my attorney. "Julie," he said, "just remember that you'll still go home at night and put on your pajamas like anybody else." At the time, I thought he'd just made an off-color joke about imagining what my colleagues looked like in pajamas. But as I started down the road with the help of my four-legged friends, I realized he was simply saying I was not so different after all—and certainly not alone.

About twenty-two million people in the United States—also divorced—were putting on their pajamas just like me.

With any significant loss I believe a large part of the difficulty lies in sorting through the feelings. And animals, ironically, often prove themselves to be our best and wisest companions. So hang onto your pajamas. Therc is life ahead. Just follow the happy tails.

—Julie Rogers

"If I were asked to give what I consider the single most useful bit of advice for all humanity, it would be this: Expect trouble as an inevitable part of life, and when it comes, hold your head high, look it squarely in the eye, and say, 'I will be bigger than you. You cannot defeat me.'"

—Ann Landers

Part I

Grief

CHAPTER 1
Separation

If, at the beginning of my journey, somebody had told me that the road met four-legged counsel at every turn, I might have raised an eyebrow. How could these creatures possibly know what I was up against? How could holding a three-day-old puppy offer the comfort and wisdom to see me through the toughest decision I'd ever made?

All I can say is, they were there, every step of the way. Hansel was my first teacher of many. Each animal and each encounter advanced me through another stage in an emotional recovery I won't forget. One step at a time, these animals walked, ran, sat, napped, and munched with me. The day I thought I'd reached the end of my rope, in fact, Hansel was there—at the other end of a nylon tracking lead, ready to show me just how wrong I was.

HANSEL

The temperature was twenty degrees. I don't remember tying a knot; I don't think I had time. I'd just set out on a three-mile run in the Texas Hill Country behind a sixty-pound Malinois named Hansel, a hardy Belgian shepherd on a mission to search and rescue. A high-energy working dog driven to please, Hansel resembled a German shepherd. We were joined by a fifteen-foot nylon lead on a drill to find his trainer, Jerry, in a seventy-five-acre pasture surrounded by woods. Hansel knew what he was doing, and I didn't.

My friends and fellow dog trainers brought me along that day, a motley bunch of all ages in down jackets, slickers, sweats, fatigues, longjohns, and ski masks. Some knew I was going through a tough time with a separation and impending divorce; just that morning I'd tried without success to reach my attorney who was parked in criminal court proceedings for the rest of the day.

So, with the coaxing of my friends, I ended up instead in the middle of a dog-training class, rolling up my jeans and stuffing what was left of my hair under a baseball cap.

Hansel's owner, Faye, handed me her pair of kidskin work gloves. I thanked her and tugged them on while someone else held the rough-and-ready Hansel.

"Jeez, it's cold," I complained.

My friends smiled at me. "Not for long," Faye said. The wind whipped her ponytail across her face. Minus her gloves, she instinctively began rubbing her hands together and blowing on them.

Hansel lunged against his harness, ready to run. I dug my heels in the ground and threw all my weight against the lead to hold him back for ten more seconds.

"Pick up your feet," Faye warned.

No joke, I thought. I'd seen too many spaghetti westerns with sunbaked cowpokes dragged halfway across Sicily.

I took a deep breath and checked the second hand on my watch. It clicked past twelve. Jerry had told me to give him seven minutes to hide, and his seven minutes were up.

"Time," I said, and gave Hansel five feet of slack. The lead snapped straight and launched me from a standstill to a dead run. I was vaguely aware of my spine cracking like popcorn as I bounded after him. Forget the chiropractor; that was the best spinal adjustment I'd had in months.

"Go, go, go!" my friends cheered from behind.

Did I have any other choice?

Hansel went, darting this way and that, nose up, nose down. His ears twitched forward and back. Steam rose off his fawn-colored fur. I could see the muscles in his hindquarters straining, yanking me onward.

I bolted after him, trying to keep enough slack in the lead to let him do his work. We circled the same bale of hay a couple of times. Topped the next hill. My right ankle took a painful twist when I misgauged the height of a crawdad mound on the descent. This wasn't any polyurethane jogging track. My breathing came harder, in short puffs of steam.

I'd considered myself to be in fairly decent shape for nearing forty, although I'd recently filled a prescription for Inderal for continuing chest pain, and had dropped twenty pounds in six weeks without trying. Hansel was easily half my weight. Two months before I could've at the very least offset his war charge. Now I was strapped on like a bouncing yo-yo.

This is it, I thought as I heaved onward. *I'm gonna croak. Right out here behind a haystack.*

As Hansel and I looped back to the starting point, my friends were still cheering us. The wind shifted. Hansel seemed confused. He slowed, his nose tacking the ground right, then left. A steady hum of blood rushed between my ears. My head was soaked in sweat. I tossed my ball cap at the group.

"I think he lost it!" I yelled. A raw north wind sliced through my hair, goading me forward with all the mercy of an ice pick. Hansel spun on a dime, bounding off in another direction.

"Not yet!" someone yelled after me.

As I sprinted after Hansel on that terribly cold day, along with the growing discomfort in my lungs and legs, I began to connect with the remarkable conduct of this dog and, be it temporarily, to forget my own misery.

A Therapeutic Experience

Prior to our run, I'd only seen Hansel as a mild-mannered dog working in a hospital setting. In addition to his search-and-rescue training, Hansel was also a therapy dog. He was part of our growing group, The Good Shepherds, that made weekly rounds to area nursing homes and hospitals—sometimes on doctor's orders—to visit patients in need of special attention. I'd seen Hansel climb into a lift chair and lay his thick muzzle across the chest of a quadriplegic named Carl, frequently expressing reluctance to leave his bedside.

Carl hadn't walked since his losing battle with multiple sclerosis began at age twenty-one. He hadn't spoken an intelligible word in three years. Save for tracking objects with his big brown eyes and occasional spastic movements, Carl might've been considered a vegetable.

I'd watched Hansel nuzzle Carl's hand and slip his nose under Carl's flaccid fingers, a gesture that always earned a hearty giggle.

For a young man like Carl, bedridden in a nursing home by the age of twenty-five, these animals were the highlight of his week. He'd roll his head from side to side and try to clap his hands.

Soon the news about these therapy visits began to spread. Our group began receiving calls from other area nursing homes, charity organizations, and the local media.

When a newspaper reporter in suit and tie, steno pad in hand—curious about the history, annals, and claims of pet therapy—followed us around one day, he was in for a surprise. We all were, for Hansel was about to perform his first miracle.

Hansel went through his usual routine with Carl and, as we prepared to leave, expressed the same reluctance to go.

The reporter was only marginally impressed. "What can pet therapy really do for a patient like Carl? Does it work? If so, does it surpass traditional therapies?"

I started to answer, but was interrupted by Carl's gurgling noises.

Hansel whined. His triangular ears stood at attention as he watched Carl.

I stepped forward, alarmed. Carl's face was growing deep red as he craned his neck off the pillow.

"I wuv him," Carl said.

A Decision

As I pumped my knees high in a boot-camp run after this remarkable dog, I realized that Hansel could work the same miracle for me. The emotional balm and internal enrichment of animals could sustain me through a sorrow that threatened to rip me in two.

Hansel, leading me by fifteen feet, lurched left and headed for the woods. His tail whipped furiously from side to side. I began retracting the line, but not before he dove into the underbrush with a yelp. Huffing, I reached the edge of the trees in time to see Hansel licking his trainer's hand.

"Good boy," Jerry said as he stood up out of the leaves and grinned at me. "Nice day for a run, huh, Jules?"

I leaned against the nearest tree. "It's turning out that way."

CHAPTER 2
Alone

The next Friday I was standing alone at the animal shelter in a roomful of cages, surrounded by deafening barks and whines, trying to make a mental note on which animals I'd missed that day. As I counted, I realized I'd exercised them all except Gigi. She was the last dog, and seemed the most alone. I was immediately sorry I hadn't gotten to her sooner. But I also knew why I hadn't. She reminded me too much of myself.

Gigi

When I pulled Gigi out of her cage, she buried her head under my arms and shivered. She was so utterly alone.

I took her into the director's office, away from ear-splitting echoes of barking, baying, and yipping in the dog area. I tried standing her on the linoleum tile floor. *Whoosh!* She went down spread-eagled, like a cartoon character.

So I laid Gigi on my lap, and my heart went out to this gangly puppy sprawled across my legs, who didn't even know how to be held. She was a foxhound-cur mix with little sorrel and white spots and soft folds of skin around the muzzle that breeders call dewlaps. She was growing up in a cage. Although she received recreation daily, her legs repeatedly collapsed underneath her.

The staff veterinarian had said he believed Gigi's weakness was more a state of mind than a physical infirmity. Gigi needed love and room to grow. She needed a good home.

I held her and cried. My first day as a volunteer at the shelter had gone pretty well until Gigi, when all the sadness came crashing down. There was too much of it here—too many lives spending long months in cages, each pressing a nose between the bars for the chance to be loved.

I knew the statistics. Many animals fared far better here in these clean, disinfected surroundings versus life in the streets. This center was new; the cages hadn't even begun to tarnish. Most animals in the shelter received better attention, stimuli, and veterinary care. Puppies like Gigi were usually quickly adopted. But even knowing that didn't stop me from hating the cages.

Gigi's was the last stop in my self-imposed sequence. I had to work that way, because they all wanted out. If I'd gone about my job in any other fashion, they all would've ended up at my house. I already had as many strays as I could afford to adopt. I had to remember my goal, to try to bring momentary joy into their lives, to do what I could.

The weather outside was a typical raw January. Pervading sleet deterred me from taking the smaller pups outside, so Gigi and I had gone into the director's office. I held her for a while, then pulled out the phone directory, trying to think of someone who would want this sweet, bashful puppy. I dialed a relative first.

"She's got a wonderful disposition. Won't be a very large dog, either."

Five calls later, my litany was still falling on deaf ears. Finding a home for a throwaway animal can be as tough as selling potty-chairs door-to-door. Nobody wants one or plans for one.

Gigi got to me. As I held her close, I think everything awful came to me then—her inevitable destiny, my inability to help her, and the ultimate failure of my first marriage.

In the school of hard knocks I've learned there are some sicknesses we can't touch, any more than we have found a twentieth century cure for cancer or a good home for every animal. Illness strikes and kills, regardless of our sincerest efforts. I had once hailed the power of the individual, the strength of one to make a difference. That was my motto when I agreed to volunteer at the shelter. On my one day off work, I'd try to make a difference.

In a relationship, though, I found out it really does take two to tango—that all the individual intensity in the world doesn't work well very long. Some of us discover this the hard way. To tango, we need the discipline and dedication of two people. It's a dance that can be performed in many ways. If I truly love someone, I will learn my part in this difficult dance—how every step matters if we're really determined to do this together. I am blessed if my partner truly feels the same way.

Being in a perpetually troubled relationship is an incredibly lonely place. Two people can sleep in the same bed, share the same interests, even go to the same workplace—but if they can't sit down and reason with one another on the simple issues, what do they really have in common? We'd begun to systematically exclude each other—to essentially live our lives alone.

I was alone.

"We're closing up," the director said through the doorway.

I started, waking Gigi, now nearly asleep in my lap.

The director's jeans were soaked from bathing animals and spraying out cages. Tufts of hair clung on her shirt. By the set of her jaw I could tell she was tired. "Any luck?"

I shook my head.

"It always takes longer than we'd like," she admitted.

As I returned Gigi to her cage and her drooping eyes stared at me from the other side, she showed me honesty about aloneness. Her sadness wasn't altogether different from my own: a hollow, empty take on what life offered at the moment, coupled with a disillusionment that kills. I remember looking back at her that day and realizing: If I was already that much alone, I might as well get honest about it, just like her. Who was I fooling?

Journey to Wisdom

It's easy to fall in love and equally easy to fall out. Eros. That's the easy-come, easy-go side of love. I feel this way today, but maybe not tomorrow. Feelings change. Illusions can reveal themselves for what they really are.

Loving someone as a pure act of will, on the other hand, can be the most difficult task you'll ever ask of yourself.

I wondered how prepared Gigi was to experience the world outside should she get the chance—this whimpering, lonesome puppy who couldn't even stand on her own legs. I remember the cautious *thump-thump* of her tail against my leg. Gigi needed someone to trust. She needed room to run. She needed a place to grow. She needed to experience real love.

I was about to strike out by myself, about to be truly alone. I, too, was in a cage of tears, pressing my nose against the bars for a chance to be loved. I started my journey there, alone and afraid.

Gigi was the beginning of my emotional recovery. She met me in her loneliness and helped me feel mine. For losing a relationship is, in essence, a death. It is a very lonely place and the most alone I've ever felt.

I was about to grieve a death, but I wasn't fully prepared for its complexity. Loss by separation or divorce is much more complicated than grieving the death of a loved one. On the surface, loss by divorce is far less noble and far more harmful.

This need not be so. All along I'd believed that the pain of reconstructing life after any great loss is what we make of it. How I chose to journey through my grief could impact new directions in my life and in my future relationships.

As I'd worked with Gigi that day, she'd shown me that the most difficult part of loss was sorting through the emotions. Grief has a way of making us sadder but wiser. We live and learn. The path to wisdom was a much deeper, more emotionally charged place than I'd ever been. In going there, I had to be willing to discover grief, take hold of it, and allow it to be my teacher.

Finding Feelings

Gigi found her way out of that cage into a warm and loving family with two children. She was up and about in no time, romping after a Koosh ball like nobody's business, pushing that soft muzzle of hers into the bellies of giggling kids. A barely detectable limp remains, which she will probably outgrow. She continues, however, to occasionally flop down and whimper for no apparent reason. Perhaps she remembers the pain of being alone.

Possibly this, too, is her unique tribute of thanks, a prayer of sorts, that she is no longer sad. I am grateful for Gigi's example about the necessity to start by being alone. Single again can be a lonely place, and I wasn't sure about going there. Who wants to admit they feel afraid and abandoned? I didn't want to be alone with myself, much less with my emotions. Who likes to feel turned upside down and inside out?

In a society that makes automatic assumptions about the wrongness of choosing to be alone, this can be a difficult choice. By and large, we are a deadly busy society. I had many ways to avoid being alone, but they did not lead to wisdom. I knew I could preoccupy myself with beneficial activities such as attending school, working, volunteering, or even joining a recovery group—but in the end, if I didn't get alone and feel my feelings, I wasn't allowing grief to give its passage. I'd shoved aside my emotions to say goodbye and therein delayed my journey to real emotional healing.

Get in touch with my feelings? No problem, I thought. I sat down to make my list—and froze. Got up, put on a pot of coffee. Sat down again. What did I feel? I felt like I was composing a dreaded essay about incontinence. Who cares about the nasty little details on that one, right? You just want to be rid of the inconvenience. Have your bladder suspended and kiss that problem goodbye.

Mine was fast becoming much more than an inconvenience. Annoyed? That's how I feel, I thought. I'd just wasted several good years of my life. Too ordinary and too humiliating to even bother feeling about. I didn't feel a thing.

So I flunked session one.

I thought about feelings some more. In the back of my mind, I could still see Gigi's droopy brown eyes peering at me through the bars. I could still feel the light, rhythmic thump-thump of her tail.

I tried a different angle. In the context of any other relationship loss I'd had, what was I supposed to feel? Confused? Angry? Sad? Guilty? Embarrassed? Lonely? Hurt? Frustrated? Ashamed? Helpless?

Did I feel betrayed? Disappointed? Overwhelmed? Exposed? Devastated? Frightened? Dumbfounded?

A friend of mine suggested that I do myself a favor by identifying my feelings early on and feeling them. *Great,* I thought, *I can't even get past comparing my divorce to incontinence.* But with time, the words began to come. I tried to find the particular shades of emotion that stirred me as well. Annoyed became exasperated. Numb became confused.

Alone became privacy. I realized I had not only the opportunity, but also the privilege of discovering my feelings alone. A place for my eyes only. I could take a bald-faced look at those emotions that set me on edge and feel them.

So I got started on those feelings.

But why alone? Being alone smacks of failure. Who's comfortable with loneliness? I was horribly afraid of being lonely.

Charlie Brown in the *Peanuts* comic strip said it well. He sat down at the psychiatrist's booth and asked Lucy if she could cure loneliness. She said for a nickel, she could cure anything. Charlie Brown elaborated, asking her if she could cure " . . . deep-down, black, bottom-of-the-well, no-hope, end-of-the-world, what's-the-use loneliness?" Lucy sputtered the clincher in bold black letters: "For the same nickel?!"

Alone is tough.

Some time passed before I discovered my greatest moments of healing while alone. Being alone allowed me time to think uninterrupted and to draw upon some candid self-esteem that I hadn't welcomed in awhile. Even with that much, I still felt strongly that my aloneness was only temporary. New companionship or remarriage wasn't out of the question. I didn't think becoming totally comfortable in my aloneness was necessary for healing.

Attending my feelings was.

Being alone is easy to avoid. Many of us are busier than we'd like to be. I later realized productivity has its place—after I'd taken the time to get in touch with the many faces of grief.

As I closed the door on a relationship and dreams I'd nurtured, the barbs of loneliness were very real and very unavoidable. Many uncertainties rose up to haunt me. Bewilderment certainly comes to mind. Recovery became a time for questioning—everything. Grief provoked me to inquire about what truths ultimately matter in life. I was forced to call into question what I'd held up as reality, and how that reality governed my world.

Would I continue operating under the assumption that I was a unique, created being living in an open system, subject to divine intervention? Or would I adopt the disturbing hypothesis of quantum physics, of a world left to chance and events occurring at random? Did sadness serve a purpose?

Taking the time to get alone and thrash out sadness and loneliness is a two-way trip. My journey to recovery began with a heartbreaking plunge to the bottom. The only way to go was up.

CHAPTER 3
Denial

When I first heard about Archie Lee, I admit I was drawn to meet him more out of morbid curiosity than genuine admiration. I simply did not believe such an animal existed. On several levels, I was about to learn how much in denial I was. So, on an unseasonably warm fall day a few weeks after my divorce was final, I paid a visit to Archie Lee—as a true doubting Thomas.

Archie Lee

Archie Lee was a cat who probably should have been euthanized. He'd been run over, an accident that had damaged his spine and had rendered him blind, sensory disoriented, arthritic, and epileptic.

His owners, however, saw an adorable eleven-year-old cat worthy of saving. They gave him the run of a beautiful house, although he often forgot where he was and went crashing into the dining room centerpiece. You could say he made their lives more—interesting.

Archie Lee got generous daily doses of antiseizure medications, anti-inflammatories, eye emollients, and any other veterinary treatments required to maintain the delicate balance that enabled him to exist.

He wasn't a particularly attractive cat. Though his mottled coat was healthy from the fastidious care it received, on first sight I thought I'd just encountered the world's first ambulatory PVC pipe. His eyes didn't focus, and he had a yowl that brought goose flesh.

For some, the thought of keeping this miserable representation of its species alive would've been a questionable venture at best, but his owners volunteered it with such joy. They weren't certain how much Archie Lee understood, but the veterinarians reassured them he wasn't in any pain.

When I first met him, Archie Lee's incredible adoptive mother, Pat, greeted me at the door, beaming. Pat, a small, quick woman with incredible energy, always has a ready smile.

Archie Lee was nowhere in sight.

"Let me see if I can find him," Pat said. She started down a long hallway leading to the back of the house. I thought I heard a faint *twang* coming from one of the bedrooms.

I sat on the sofa in the living room. Pat was still talking from the hall. "He sometimes forgets what part of the house he's in."

Just outside a bay window to my right, there was painters' scaffolding pushed up against a tree. *Twang.* The air conditioner clicked on.

Something in the vents, I thought. "You all doing some remodeling, Pat?"

Pat appeared at the door, still minus Archie Lee.

I'd clearly interrupted her train of thought. I pointed outside.

"Oh!" She grinned. "That's Archie Lee's. We keep it up there for retrieving him off the roof." She went back down the hall. *Twang.*

"What's that noise?" I called after her.

"Not sure yet," she called back.

Minutes later I heard Pat laughing from one of the bedrooms. "Archie Lee! What are you doing inside this mattress?"

Cycles

We stand at this threshold of aging, deterioration, and death almost every day asking: Is the wreckage worth saving? Can something good rise from the ruins? Does this really matter? Do we have the right to extend life using a respirator? The right to pull the plug? When is continuing life no longer living?

The act of salvaging a relationship on the rocks can be an equally dubious process, requiring hours and days and years of cyclic tedium. In a healthy relationship, the act of loving is circular—by extending myself to nurture, I grow to extend again. The act of destroying a relationship is circular as well.

For the most part, my first marriage maintained the same irreconcilable differences to the very end, and we continued to argue about the same problems. While we recognized the inefficiency of repeating the same argument, we did it anyway—and more frequently under duress. The adage "familiarity breeds contempt" is true, especially during an old argument. I later learned that arguing in circles—the very cyclic nature of the pattern itself—serves to protect us from anxieties surrounding change. We'd go round and round but never come around to resolving anything, for that would mean we might have to undergo a dreaded change.

In a relationship, change can mean many things, both positive and negative—from spiritual growth to emotional decline, from financial stability to bankruptcy court, from renewed vigor to irreversible disease, from winner-takes-all to an ultimate sacrifice. The process of salvaging a relationship is dubious because the cycles of loving and destroying often overlap. I may apply myself to extending real love on Monday—only to blow it all away in the same old argument on Friday.

One of the most consistent and pervasive arguments in my first marriage revolved around my desire to work at home. I wanted to take a night course in medical transcription and set up my service under independent contracts. To do that, I needed extra time, money, and energy. Although I enjoyed my job as an athletic director, the hours were odd and long. We also needed my income to make ends meet.

The harder I pushed to scrape together the means to make my dream come true, the more I resented having to do this around a full-time job. Many of my attempts to save money backfired—like not cutting my hair for five years. I started having headaches at work. They'd always start the same way, a dull throb behind my eye sockets, like a sinus headache.

I was on the phone, trying to work out an employee's scheduling conflict, at the same time longingly poring over the community college calendar and considering my slim chances for enrolling in night school.

"Hang on just a minute," I finally said. I put the phone on hold and looked at the employee schedule in vain for a possible replacement. I couldn't have this employee on lifeguard duty and teaching aerobics simultaneously. She knew that. I knew that. At the same time I was tugging at an industrial-strength scrunch band that held my ponytail in place.

Back on the line, I offered my best shot. "If you're willing to take the next holiday, I might be able to work something out."

Not exactly what this employee wanted to hear. Finally, "Well, sure. If that's all you can do."

A moment of uneasy silence. I looked at the employee schedule for what seemed the fiftieth time. Chucked the college calendar in the trash. *God, it hurt to blink.*

"You all right?"

The sound of genuine concern in her voice surprised me. "Do I sound that bad?"

"Kinda strung out."

"It's allergies."

"Oh."

At that fated moment, my scrunch band snapped in two with a *ping* and flew across the room.

"Jeez!" I fumbled the receiver back to my ear.

"What was that?" I heard her asking.

The relief was instantaneous. The weight of my ponytail, quite simply, was killing me. "My headache," I said.

Degeneration and decline, especially in a relationship, are difficult to acknowledge. I could not accept it at first—this Archie Lee tottering around in our lives, so painful to embrace. But he was there—distinct, feeble, and dying. Our relationship was dying from the inside out. I had vowed to accept the bad with the good. The new with the old. Two into one. I was committed. I had vowed for life.

This couldn't be happening. Not to me.

The Faces Of Denial

Much later I came to realize that the Archie Lees I chose to perpetuate, whether out of need, pity, or mercy—must eventually go to the ground. Our marriage was following its course to a natural death. We came to a place where we would continue forever to emotionally separate. I knew if I remained in an unhealthy relationship in the pretense of something good to come, I would end up leaving anyway. Death comes regardless.

Denial is the seed that has to fall to the ground: life to death to life again. Denial is a pacifier for shock and disbelief about a dying relationship. I had to plow through it for a time, with disbelief serving as my shock absorber.

The concept of making a clean break from a once intimate relationship is a neatly packaged misnomer and a paradox that drums up denial. I knew I might as well forget about the concept of a clean break: for us, it didn't exist.

Our intimacy, repeatedly maimed by manipulation and enabling, became distorted over time. For the better part of the marriage, I was unaware of any manipulation taking place. I simply didn't identify certain behavior as manipulative, even when others pointed it out to me. I didn't see that even my attempts to "help" were attached to an underlying agenda for regaining control.

During the first shock waves of divorce, I hailed the original intimacy—the young, undamaged Archie Lee. It was difficult to observe how far away we'd come from something good, but we had. Day-in, day-out slights, following our own self-interests at the expense of the other, and continually attempting to pick up the pieces of each other's personal dilemmas all eroded away our intimacy. We were no longer partners in a true and healthy way, nor could our intimacy be restored.

Even with the anatomy of a dying intimacy peeled back before my eyes, I still didn't want to see it. So I drummed up denial.

Part of the denial process, ironically, is denying one's own involvement. I might say, "I'm not the one who wants this. You're destroying this relationship." Denying my involvement in the death process of a relationship might be convenient, but we both know that's not the way relationships work.

Denial gave me time to disengage, to mourn. In a society with access to so many instant services, some people might expect themselves to disengage at least quickly, if not instantaneously. Denial tells me that for relationships, this isn't so. Therefore, "in denial" is not a bad place to be. It's a bad place to stay. While I hang onto the Archie Lees, I'm essentially hanging onto myself, and all that I've invested in a partnership. But eventually I had to face our relationship's frailness, albeit at my own pace, and let it go.

Denial also worked on me another way. About the time I was ready to accept the inevitability of our divorce, I heard a little voice on my left shoulder:

" 'ey, quick chick! So what's the problem, mon?"

On the average, I don't hear voices. I try to calmly and logically think things through. Perhaps my imagination was working overtime, I don't know. On a scale of one to ten, I think I rated about nine for stress and exhaustion. For a while I tried ignoring these little guys, but they were very persistent.

Before I could answer, I got a rejoinder from my right:

"Tiko! You everlovin' cheap thrill! Ain't you supposed to be in Jamaica?"

"This lady, she killin' me, mon. She think she got it tough—"

"Shut up, Tiko."

I was wondering, *Who's Tiko?*

"Ah, he's just your average denial junkie. Our tax dollars at work. Supposed to be doing thirty-to-life in jail in Jamaica. Don't listen to him."

"She don't know what she doin', mon. It ain't that bad."

So it ain't, huh? Will somebody please tell me where Tiko gets his information?

"Oh, right. Like she made all this up."

"Would I lie to you?"

"Yeah, yeah. Just like you didn't mule Gonja out of that fishing boat in Montego Bay."

"It was a Sea-Doo, mon."

"He'll be done in a minute."

As days go, I'd had a fairly sane one until Tiko came along.

" 'ey, I tellin' you, mon. Him and her, they's happenin' if she want it to."

Really? You work miracles, too?

"Jeez! Don't listen to him."

I'm trying not to.

"They got no problem, mon."

"Yeah, just like you, huh, Tiko? Hey, don't listen—"

I *was* listening. *I really don't need this right now.*

"Damn right, you don't. Beat it, Tiko."

That wasn't the last I heard from Tiko or the feisty voice on my left who chose to remain anonymous. Denial is a very persuasive and protective force. Deciphering reality from nonreality was a daily slugfest between my shoulder-to-shoulder contenders for a while. Tiko tried to minimize problems and accentuate the possibility that things could somehow take a turn for the better. On certain days, I found it terribly difficult not to believe him.

Denial is, after all, part of coming to terms with the truth.

I think often about Archie Lee and his owners, who remained valiant in their effort to support him in his infirmities. I observed the joy this brought for a while, to keep this animal from dying. In time, however, Archie Lee had to go down, along with all the efforts put forth in keeping him alive and well.

With the same dramatic irony that surrounded his everyday life, Archie Lee heard the automatic garage door open one afternoon, and, as his routine went, ran pell-mell across the yard to meet Pat's husband, full-speed ahead into the porch banister. His neck snapped and he died instantly. Pat told me the story with laughter in her voice, but tears in her eyes. This can be an extremely difficult task, to bury the living past.

CHAPTER 4
Blame

Part of the enjoyment of my family reunions has always been sharing our various and sundry pets. One of our collective critters, Snickers, brings smiles with him every time. As dogs go, he truly lives up to his name. He knows how to have fun and how to find trouble. With trouble comes punishment, or taking blame—one of his veritable pastimes, it seems. He shrugs off a scolding with such dignity, then humors himself by finding more trouble.

Blame was a far greater albatross to me than to Snickers. Until I learned how blame functioned to carry me forward and how to let it go, I was angry.

SNICKERS

Snickers, a long-haired dachshund and anthropomorphic cousin, had the uncanny ability to understand complete sentences in English or Spanish, which always fascinated me. By the time he was just six years old, he possessed an amazing vocabulary.

Snickers lived in the swimming pool during the summer, taking belly flops off the diving board while barking nonstop. He would stand in line with the children for his turn on the diving board. By the end of summer, his sorrel hair would bleach out to a patented sand blond and frizz:

a very bad rendition of, but likeness to, Tina Turner's comeback 'do.

Snickers, like any other kid having his fun, sometimes didn't know when to quit. I was lounging on a pool float in the shallow end one day, watching the children and Snickers, when my cousin, Dori, came yelling to poolside like all-out war.

"Snickers! *Salte del agua!* Now!"

I looked around. The children grew very quiet. In the deep end, Snickers surfaced with a Splash Bomb ball fast between his jowls.

"What's wrong?" I asked. I threw some water on my face. That day, as I remember it, was a scorcher.

"His bladder," Dori said. She was very pregnant at the time, teetering over the edge. I held my breath.

She snatched Snickers out of the pool and held him at arms' length. "He can't hold it like he used to. You didn't see the water change color, *no?*"

I very quickly retracted my arm from the water. Everybody was jumping out of the pool. During repeated dives for his ball, Snickers had taken in too much pool water. His belly looked like the Goodyear blimp ready to launch. He had, in fact, *launched* a good bit already during his last dive, immediately detected by a chemical water treatment that changes color in the presence of urine.

I often worried, however, that we expected too much from Snickers. He seemed almost too human. Thus when he came up with those certain doggy habits, our first instinct was to shame them out of him.

This is one of the fine lines in love, I think—to bring out the best in a person while letting one be all that one is. It is a juxtaposition of attitudes: Do I praise Snickers for his capability to swim underwater and scold him when he drips on the carpet? Does my degree of intolerance match the violation? In the outcome, does his motive really matter if I'm set on blaming him anyway? When a relationship is in trouble, how much blaming will it take before we recognize the fear and hurt underneath?

For a while, I looked to blame as a pragmatic way of answering my most confusing questions about the dissolution of a relationship once valuable to me. Blame games became my futile attempts to solve one of life's toughest riddles, or how lovers fall out of love. My blaming walked hand in hand with a mixed bag of emotions that included fear, hurt, anger, disappointment, and shock. By blaming, I kept my cool. I cut my losses and stuffed them into a blame bag. For the moment, I didn't have to feel the hurt and the anger boiling underneath.

A Blame Game

I suppose none of our problems would've come to a head if we'd done our dishes by hand. But we had this dishwasher—and that was the beginning of the end. You think I'm kidding, but I'm not. Our dishwasher started a blame game.

I load a dishwasher pretty much like I do everything else—on the run. On my way out the door (usually running late), I crack open the dishwasher door just enough to drop my cereal bowl on the top rack. It's neither systematic nor functional. It's called not being late for work.

Later on my soon-to-be ex, Sully, comes through (sometimes running late), cracks open the dishwasher door, and finds all the front spots taken. So he leaves the dishes in the sink. I come home after work, infuriated by the dirty dishes.

"Cockroaches," I say. "We're breeding cockroaches."

"The problem wouldn't exist," Sully says, "if you'd stop loading the dishwasher from the front. How long do you think it takes to pull out the drawer and load from the back?"

"Same amount as it does to leave the dishes in the sink," I say.

As silly and innocuous as it sounds, this is the anatomy of a blame game. The dishwasher was a preamble of things to come. Hurt and disappointed that my spouse was unwilling to meet me halfway, I'd take over the dishes. Maybe he'd feel guilty, I'd think. And as long as neither of us was responsible or creative enough to come up with a better solution, blaming seemed to work just fine. But guess what? Those arguments about the dishwasher took a helluva lot longer than the extra four or five seconds it took either of us to load from the back. And blame games also served us in avoiding underlying problems: anger, insecurities, hurt, guilt, and fear.

Faultfinding, especially in the company of curious listeners, seems to have a respectability of working toward a solution. And sometimes it does. But mostly, faultfinding became an adversarial tool with which I colored our relationship and engaged in a good amount of mental masturbation. I wanted my roast-my-ex consortium to agree with me about how correct and concerned and captive and crushed I was by our relationship difficulties. When my friends told me that I was the straighter-than-an-arrow, on-the-up-and-up, along-the-dotted-line kind of person I believe I am, then I came away fully indulged and completely satisfied.

But wait a minute! Could I be missing something here? Let's backtrack to the dishwasher. Could it be that I possibly failed to take into account that (drumroll, please) we both contributed to the problem? Could it be that we both were at fault?

Who, me?

Not bloody well something I'd like to own up to, but so altogether necessary when it comes to healing. I knew I could continue to throw my skewer parties and serve up some well-done ex-kabob down under, or I could come right out of the closet and put a few coals on the fire for myself.

Ending a relationship usually isn't completed without much of the same anger that brought us to the end. We nurture and build; we sever and kill. In the face of such seemingly wasted effort, it's no mystery that I felt angry and no wonder I blamed. I locked into blame as a dual struggle to cope and understand. But anger is a trapdoor spider. Left to its own, anger weaves a deathtrap, a bitter disposition fueled by the resentment of being hurt and the fear of being hurt again.

Anger can take on many forms. A friend of mine used to mow his yard on the day the alimony payment was due, whether the grass needed it or not. The madder he was, the longer he'd mow. Take out a hedge, maybe a tree or two, save the mailbox for next month.

It's hard to get past anger.

Anger for the short term, however, is a healthy response. Anger can serve, much like denial, to protect us from pain. The problem with anger, however, is that it is inherently inactive. When I blame, I assign responsibility to others, not to myself. When I'm angry, I'm really saying, "It's not my problem." I'm emotionally so locked into reacting that I cannot objectively see that others often interact with my own behavior (ah, the dishwasher again), or as a result of the way I behave toward them.

In the big picture, I had to realize I arrive where I am by the degree of responsibility I'm willing to assume in any area in life. The extent to which people will go to avoid assuming responsibility for their own personal problems sometimes borders on ridiculous. I'd walked on that border.

In the long run, anger isn't equipped to enlighten me about the complexities of life.

Anger cannot see ten years hence how I might laugh at today's perplexity. Blame cannot look into a faltering relationship and navigate me through a maze of complicated turns and sequences.

As long as I allowed anger to guide me, I was so busy attempting to assign blame where blame was due, I failed to see that getting beyond the finger-pointing meant the freedom to love again.

One day I finally realized that if complete recovery was my objective, I had to let anger serve its purpose and let it go. For me, letting go of anger and blame was a passage into the same pure exhilaration Snickers must feel when he bounds off the diving board and soars high above the water.

CHAPTER 5
Negotiations

The dimensions this little fellow added to my life remain nothing less than miraculous. Our first family pet, Woodrow, was a kitten no longer than five inches head to tail when I brought him home from the shelter. I don't think I consciously selected him as a bargaining chip, but he was. Sully was partial to cats, and I to dogs. That trip to the shelter changed my mind, and a large part of my destiny.

Woodrow

Many caregivers describe adopting an animal as an urgent experience. At any given moment, a little life somewhere slips away, and intuition coupled with adequate preparation can indeed save souls. Such urgency can be strong enough to wrest us from our workaday routine and plant us in front of an animal crate.

I can't say I was exactly rooted to the spot on my first trip to the Dallas Society for the Prevention of Cruelty to Animals; the building itself is a huge maze of rooms, cages, and species. The cat area spanned at least three rooms, with many compatible animals paired and tripled in cages. *So many . . . so many,* I thought, as I wandered from room to room.

Woodrow was the tiny little alley tom I first overlooked. He was in a cage with five other kittens, sitting off by himself, his head sunk low between his forepaws.

I hailed a worker sweeping with a push broom nearby. "May I look at this one?" I'd also noticed a blue band around the kitten's neck. "What does that mean? He's not already taken, is he?"

Since my questioning had rapidly turned more complicated, the worker stalled. He looked fresh out of high school and a little confused. "Let me go find out," he said.

I mentally chastised myself while he was gone. *Jeepers, don't jump out of your skin. It's not a crisis.*

But it was. The entire building with its pine disinfectant masking smells of urine, the constant whines and mewls of animals in confinement, and the scurrying handful of workers *screamed* crisis.

The boy was back, pushing past me toward the cage. "This one's still available." He popped open the door, swept the other kittens aside as they charged forward, and plucked up Woodrow out of the corner.

Woodrow settled in the crook of my arm, in the folds of my coat, like he'd always belonged. I think he embodied all of the adoration, charm, and pity I'd ever felt. My emotional ties to Woodrow were purely and amazingly instantaneous.

I scratched between his ears with an index finger—all that would fit on his tiny head—and was surprised to feel the faint hum of purring before I actually heard it. When I had to momentarily put him back to fill out paperwork, he dove at the cage door with mewls of protest.

Two days later, Woodrow stopped purring. As I watched him try to climb into his litter box, or take a drink from the smallest cat bowl I could find (soon replaced by even smaller lids off margarine tubs), or bat about the nubby cat balls I'd bought, I grew more and more concerned. He just didn't seem to have the normal energy of a kitten. By the third day, I'd had all I could stand. I took him to the veterinarian.

On initial examination, the veterinarian explained to me that Woodrow was indeed sick; they'd need to run some tests on him. Woodrow's illness, he said, might range from a treatable flu to a malformed liver to cancer.

"If his tests show infection consistent with flu, we'll treat him with antibiotics and try to get him to eat," the veterinarian explained. He was a tall, gangly fellow who practically bent himself in two to study, through his soda-bottle-thick bifocals, the tiny Woodrow on the exam table. He hesitated. "Then again, we see an animal occasionally with a missing kidney, or another vital organ in the wrong place." He frowned. "There's not much we can do about that."

After two days of treatment, the veterinarian informed me Woodrow still refused to eat. His chances didn't look good.

I cried harder for that little animal than I have for any other creature I've ever known. I later came to see, however, that I mourned for much more than a little mucky gray cat I'd turned out from the shelter.

Adopting Woodrow was one in a long string of negotiations I made in my first marriage, hoping to keep things together in that relationship. *The perfect Christmas present for Sully,* I'd thought.

That year, Woodrow was. By his third day at the veterinarian's, Woodrow had taken a turn for the better and had begun to eat. By the week's end, he was home again and working wonders between us. He assuaged underlying tension in our relationship with many smiles. Woodrow's kitty mischief—whether getting lodged inside a coat's sleeve after a growing spurt, or growling with the lions in the television movie *Ben Hur*—kept us laughing. He was a gift that by design said, *I want to give you something precious because you're special to me.* For a time, Woodrow elicited reconciliation between us.

Much later I realized I was negotiating for changes that couldn't happen. I finally conceded that it's humanly impossible to undo the damage in someone else's past, to heal problems that continue to torment, to empower another to be or do what he or she can't envision or bring about.

It's only natural to try. I think most people want to experience happiness, which means surrounding themselves, for the most part, with people who are happy. I want my loved ones to be happy.

A relationship, even when good, can be stripped down to a series of negotiations. People nudge and move each other every day. Most people become accustomed to the process of negotiating with the ones they love on a daily basis.

When a relationship turns sour, the inclination is to turn up the heat, to lobby for changes. Some people are more disinclined than others to let go, even after negotiations are no longer healthy or effective.

Up to that point, I'd pressed for options; I'd held on to hopes and expectations that things could work out. I'd lobbied for a sick and dying relationship with the same raw initiative I had when I took Woodrow to the veterinarian's office and pressured the vet to do everything he could.

Complicated Bargaining

In a separation due to death, the negotiating stage is less complex. Memories and loyalties to a deceased spouse can fade with time. Nothing remains to negotiate.

Ending a relationship through separation or divorce is complicated by the fact that both partners are still alive. Wounds run deep. One or both feel rejected. In edging past the hurt, both parties may be left sifting through layers and layers of guilt. The process of legal negotiations alone, especially when children are involved, may reopen the bartering tables off and on for years.

It's important to distinguish between the negotiations two people will make for the sake of their children and the bargaining chips they reserve for themselves. At some point they must declare negotiating—the hope for reuniting—finished.

This can be difficult, since one party may continue trying to reconcile and may even successfully win more time with further negotiations. Children may get caught up in the process—even pitting one parent against the other with disputes about visitation and monetary support in hopes of rekindling love negotiations among their parents.

I knew until I could kiss goodbye any other "maybes" that washed up in my imagination about reuniting, I wouldn't be able to shut down my side of the bargaining table. I know now that I should've shut down my side sooner. If I had it to do over again, I would've been far less ambivalent about my decision to part. I would've turned down conciliatory phone calls and meetings, because by that time it was too late.

But I kept looking for somebody else to carry the burden of choice, and that somebody never came. I didn't see the terrible harm my evasiveness inflicted as I strung along Sully with false hopes. I thought that by putting off the ultimate decision to part, I was somehow being gracious!

Calling it quits is complicated as well by the fact that while an ex-partner is still alive, the mere existence of this person can, even on a subconscious level, reinstate the possibility of reuniting. I learned the hard way: this is not the time to indulge yourself in second thoughts!

Negotiating a breakup is difficult. Throwing in the towel on a once-intimate relationship has all the optimism of losing. Most people don't like finding themselves in a position to bail. The decision to quit a relationship is a difficult one, no doubt about it. From an early age, most of us have been taught that quitters are losers. The truth is, while quitting can perpetuate some problems, it ends others. Knowing when to quit often keeps winners winning.

Quitting Smarts

The nature of Woodrow's recovery and his capacity to live pain-free with the awareness that he was loved constituted the humaneness of my decision—if, or when, to quit. I came to realize it's not always wrong to quit; sometimes, in fact, it's just plain smart.

In deciding whether to quit, the reality that I found myself even seriously considering ending my marriage at all indicated some level of intolerance and irreversibility in the ranks. My own self-preservation, as well, was tied into knowing when to quit: if there was any mistake to be made, I knew, many people err in favor of hanging on too long.

The most difficult aspect of negotiating is that it recycles all the questioning necessary in bringing us to the decision to split in the first place. I came full circle to where I started—several times.

Much later I realized that rescuing Woodrow, in all its emotionality and uncertainty, contained stark elements of logic, reality, and choice. When I later dissected the events of that week, I saw—though obscured by desperation at the time—that I'd left relatively little to chance. For Woodrow's safety and well-being, I'd carefully considered all the options and knew where I drew the line. When I looked again, the pointers in my human relationship were every bit as revealing and absolute. I had to let go.

Too Little Too Late

Woodrow lived to grow into a corpulent seventeen pounds and terrorize every four-legged creature in the neighborhood. He brought laughter we otherwise wouldn't have had. With Woodrow, I bargained for life and won.

I parted ways with Woodrow when my marriage ended, for he, after all, was a gift to Sully. I keep his picture on my refrigerator and think often about that tenuous week the vet force-fed that little gray mite of ours, a baby barely tipping the needle on a postage scale. Sully and I were willing to explore any options or last-ditch efforts to restore Woodrow to health, to give him the chance to grow old with us. We were willing to do or pay anything.

So what happened when it came to us? We essentially walked through that same week in slow motion all over again with our own future. The impending death of our relationship re-enacted all the original urgency and attention with which I snatched Woodrow from the shelter. But for us, highest hopes and dreams had been reduced to a penny ante trade-off. It was too late.

Negotiating—*Stuff*

If I had it to do over again in those final and preponderant legal negotiations, I would've lobbied harder for the two-pronged extension cord, the reversible king dust ruffle, and the hose hangout. Ah, the lists. Lawyer's offices are familiar with them. Sometimes I wonder what goes through a legal secretary's mind as she drafts a division of property: *Hmm—Elvis TV trays (4), two-way egg timer—what's this? Center section of the sectional couch?*

These negotiations are somewhat like hanging out your underwear in the produce department of a supermarket: exposing, and potentially disgusting. An attorney's office couldn't ask for better entertainment in the endless piles of transcripts and documents. It's like a 70 percent off table the day after Thanksgiving—a mad, mad raid. Bonkers. Ruthless.

But, hey, when everything's said and done and it means your stuff out there—from the worthless sentiments shoved in the backs of drawers to the priceless heirlooms ostentatiously displayed behind glass—property divisions can bring out the wacko in anybody. So our last negotiations, ironically, are more like fending off a mugger with a can of whipped cream. You both get creamed, anyway.

Back to that two-pronged extension cord. Do you realize how difficult it is these days to buy a two-pronged extension cord? It's fast becoming an antique. Virtually useless, but nonetheless a sentiment of the past. And that reversible king dust ruffle should come in handy (like I'm really going to rotate my king mattress every other week). The hose hangout? Now there's a very useful commodity, if you have a hose. I'm not sure whether I got the hose (I'm still looking).

When a relationship is reduced to *stuff* and that stuff comes up for grabs, it's no surprise what terrible, awful negotiators we become. Even if I never serve another meal with The King of Rock'n'Roll, it's the concept, right? *It's my stuff. Signal to control tower. I am master of all I survey.*

A Word About Cooperation

On the other hand, there's still the possibility that through the thick and thin, or in traversing the inner sanctum of nitty-gritty, I've learned a wee bit more about the importance of effective and loving negotiations, or how to really share my life with someone. For at the heart of all loving negotiations is a given called cooperation.

Lessons in cooperation usually start in early childhood. The symbolic umbilical cord thins, and while a toddler is learning that he's a separate being from his parents, he also begins receiving messages about cooperation. Much of the way I cooperate with others, especially a spouse, originates with how my parents interacted with me to enlist my cooperation.

Some people avoid conflict at great costs. Others railroad their way through life no matter what the costs. I am marching to some old drums, therefore, as I choose how I negotiate in adulthood.

I can't overemphasize the importance of acquiring effective cooperation skills. Without the capability to cooperate as a foundation, effective negotiating with your partner will always be, at best, very difficult. Part of the challenge in changing how I negotiate is recognizing just how subtle and pervasive childhood is.

With cooperation as a baseline, other effective negotiating guidelines can only further enhance a relationship:

1) Be willing. Try any change for a reasonable amount of time.
2) Be flexible. If this change proves ineffective, unfair, or otherwise harmful to the partnership or family unit, agree to discontinue it.
3) Be honest. Get assertive about what you are willing and able to do.
4) Be positive (especially with criticism). Remember: negativity kills.
5) Be kind. Attitude is everything.
6) Be thoughtful. You are not alone. Think before you act.
7) Be reasonable. Sacrificing personal health and wellbeing isn't beneficial for anyone.

Negotiating with those I love—when conducted mutually, effectively, frequently, and lovingly—will not need to resort to last-ditch strategies. When the desire to cooperate with my mate prompts the majority of my behavior, much of the work of loving is already done.

CHAPTER 6
Turning Point

A few weeks later at the shelter, I found a dog named George in the isolation unit because there were no large cages left in front. He was already in a sense being filed away—and he knew it.

My focus up to this point was about making a difference, a change. I was headed for changes all right—but they weren't exactly what I'd expected. I'd braced myself for emotional fallout, but nothing could prepare me for rock bottom. The possibility of failure hadn't occurred, either, because I'd longed so to turn things around for these animals—for George—and for myself.

George

My farewell to my former relationship wouldn't have been complete without the time I spent with George. He was a Dalmatian-Labrador mix, of gentle temperament and quiet spirit. He had a regal black coat with hints of spots, much like a black leopard. I always felt George deserved a better name, but, after all, he was burdened with many other undesirables by the time he was only two.

During the week George was forced to live in quarantine, the staff and volunteers gave him more recreation in an attempt to lift his spirits. When I took him to the recreation yard that day, he came immediately back to me and laid his head in my lap as I knelt.

Most of the dogs I took outside had bad cases of cabin fever; they were ready to romp. The center had tug-of-war ropes and old tennis balls just for that purpose. I ran my hand into my pocket for a toy, but George was simply too sad to play. I scratched behind his ears instead.

"Did you know Dalmatians have many lives?" I whispered to him. "It's true. One for every spot. And I see lots of wonderful living under there."

My heart went out to George in his distress. He was an outcast, unwanted and unwelcome in the normal course of life. In some ways, he was a prisoner to the mere sin of existence. But for that day—at that moment—I could wrap my arms around his huge neck and tell him he was really okay.

I didn't know what the next day would bring for George. I truly hoped for the very best in life for him, but I was not the one to give it. I was not the one to take him on but for more than a few brief visits at the shelter. My best was in reassuring him that he had a place on earth just as decidedly as anyone else.

George was in the low of lows. We both sat in the recreation yard that day, overwhelmed by our sadness, pain, and the uncertainty of our future.

Bottoming Out

George was adopted and returned two times to the shelter because he wasn't housebroken. Eventually, however, he was acquired by a hunting club. With training,

George was soon their star retriever. His Dalmatian's stride—almost twice the length of a full-sized Labrador—made him especially keen in the swamps, where ducks were plentiful.

I tell you this about George because, as I found him—bottomed-out in the confines of an isolation unit in a shelter—made it difficult, if not impossible, to recognize such potential. He was totally vulnerable to the circumstances that surrounded him, as well as the pain of his own isolation. The turning point for George was the arrival of an owner prepared to accept him with his negative traits and accentuate the positive.

So there I found myself at my lowest point, with all the negotiations over, no more maybes, the whole world as my carrot and too submerged in sadness to care. That was my turning point. I was puzzled by mixed feelings of vulnerability, pain, sadness, and relief. I was startled by the reality of it's over, the pain of no more, and the clarity of starting again.

Perhaps this stage might be better described as a series of turning points, or at least in terms of bearing up emotionally, the way it developed for me. I knew I was fooling myself if I expected to sail through a separation and goodbye without much of the same disbelief, vulnerability, sadness, and pain that had followed me there. In some ways, I felt no further along than when I'd started.

George was a touchdown encounter—a place where I slowly stopped relying on anything more than the step in front of me. I piloted my course for the best I could be on any given day. Some days, the weather wasn't too great.

In the "low of lows" is not the place to make life-changing decisions. I tried not to make any more choices than absolutely necessary to complete the process of separation and divorce. At the bottom, I was tempted to go for anything—a better job, another degree, a relocation—anything fresh and new for gaining a measure of anonymity, for the satisfaction of knowing that this pain was taking me somewhere, and for the security of labeling any of these external improvements as yielding a better life on my own. But life changes are not in and of themselves turning points; change for the sake of change can't be forced in order to escape pain or loneliness.

On the one hand, I was relieved by my newfound freedom to make my own choices, as well as the liberty to be my own person again. On the other, I was vulnerable to the consequences of those choices, and sad that I was facing them alone. Invariably, I was about to go through a series of life changes, and some, whether I liked it or not. Perhaps I would be able to balance my checkbook. Perhaps I wouldn't . . .

Makeovers

Life changes. I don't have any raw statistics, but my experience tells me that among the industries most likely to net real profit in the wake of a divorce, automobile dealerships, beauticians, and plastic surgeons rank right up there at the top. (I think I can get some mileage in here.)

Out with the old, in with the new. Closure. Is it any wonder I might get a little carried away? There's a certain level of comfort in a comeback, the capability to bring back the old Sal or Sue I used to know—back and better than before! Friends and foes alike will spread the news like today's headlines. "My gawd, have you seen Sue lately? Lovely ear tuck! Just the right amount."

Now don't get me wrong. Personal improvement is good. And it doesn't have to appear in the tidal wave of a divorce, either. But, as divorces go, don't I halfway expect to see some improvement? It's like an unwritten law in the textbook of marriage termination: I must show official signs of a personal makeover in progress or everybody will assume I got what I deserved!

Yeow! Hello, cruel world.

Have you ever noticed how women dish it right out there, while men use a kind of code language? "Old Sal came out all right. Just bought him a brand-new doublewide and that outboard he's been talkin' about for months now."

Hmm. So, however you name it, I'm okay with making those life changes I've been putting off for years and years, for the lack of loving support or time or money or all three.

"I still may not have the money, and I sure as hell don't have the loving support, but I've got the time now, and I do it in the name of change! For if I don't change now, my chance may never roll around again! My friends might stop calling!"

(As you can tell, some very probable and ridiculous anxieties can grow out of simple efforts to do something good for yourself.)

"Yep, I better go for that full-body dermabrasion and lip exfoliation or they'll never notice!"

I look back at some of the personal enhancements I made (sea-blue toenails, for one) and have to wonder, *Where was I?* Most people start with their heads, right? New 'do, a hint of highlights. *Nothing too garish; this is supposed to make me look better, please* (given that I went with sea-blue, I'm glad I started with my feet).

So my nail technician pulled out her color palette one day and showed me the best summertime colors she had to offer. Great-looking corals, sunflower yellows, you name it. *But look at that blue!* Had I ever seen anything like it? *Yeah—in a toilet bowl.* After throwing a couple of those little drop-ins in the tank.

Now. That was some blue. I didn't even have to go shopping. I just pointed.

Looking back, I wouldn't recommend too many decisions that require merely a wave of the index finger. But if you do decide shock factor is in order (overriding anything sensible your mother ever taught you), may I suggest a pedicure with blue nail polish? It's amazing how many people notice your feet. Add a pair of noisy flip-flops and they'll look right down there. "Splendid nail color, dahling. You've never done this before, have you?"

Ah, the changes. They're something about doing what I've wanted to do for a long time, and nothing about the true turning point. On the low end, it's a buzz at an outlet mall salon and a chain saw. On the high end, a nose job and a fast (red) sports car.

"But hey, I'm making a statement here. I'm getting past the tears, and the best is yet to come!"

A Silver Lining

From my vantage point at the bottom, I could only dream of a silver lining. I kept living in the same house and going to the same job. But I learned never to discount the power of dreams. I dreamed of finding a good mate. I dreamed of writing this book.

I also learned not to expect too much from myself at the bottom. Unlike George, my bottoming out was lined with opportunities. I had a choice. I could make my life a dungeon or a launching pad. With that turn, I left behind memories—good and bad—and moved on.

I looked into George's eyes and saw that life doesn't always resolve fairly or even gracefully. I give to my capacity, and too many times, it isn't enough. If a relationship doesn't work, it doesn't work. I must give up George to a destiny higher than me, a Maker who crossed our paths for a time, and gave me the grace to love him.

CHAPTER 7
Understanding

The next Friday at the shelter brought Quando. A German shepherd, Quando was a lucky one, in terms of his chances for adoption. But Quando, as I came to see, was unlucky in his own way, because, much like me, he didn't understand the circumstances surrounding him. He'd just lost the only master he'd ever known.

Quando

Della was a widow, and Quando, her companion of five months. An extensive illness and impending surgery made her fear for her ability to care for him. So she let him go.

Quando was beautiful, predominantly black with a uniformity of brown, fawn, and silver. He appeared well adjusted. I told her so, and she began to cry. Della, with a head full of white hair, was clearly in pain as she shuffled—her fingers clutching the roof of her station wagon for support—to the back hatch to let him out. She'd insisted on bringing Quando herself, to give him a proper goodbye. What she did for him that day, I think, was a marvelous act of human kindness. But it took great courage on both their parts.

I have watched several women become widows. Some women, like Quando's master, become physically unable to care for the dying men in their lives. Sometimes these women are forced to give up caring for their husbands long before they actually become widows.

But Quando was very healthy, young, and alive. I took him to the recreation yard where he plowed circles for two hours nonstop, restless and wary. He couldn't understand what had happened to his master. I think he sensed Della was ill, but he had no way of knowing what this ultimately meant for him.

A breed known to be bold but cautious of strangers, the German shepherd can have difficulty transferring its obedience and loyalty to a new owner. Quando finally hunkered against the fence, allowed a leash to be slipped over his neck, and returned to his cage.

Examining the Reasons

Animal shelters are full of reasons. Buried in every tripartite application form are the many reasons owners declare themselves no longer capable of caring for their pets. Not all animals in the shelter have problems. I soon realized that the reasons I saw there were not only about them, but also very much about us.

Of utmost importance to me was taking the time to examine and evaluate my reasons for walking away from a relationship. Without reasons, I couldn't begin to move beyond feelings of loss.

Sometimes there are no good reasons. For example, in an environment that supports quantum physics—the hypothesis of events happening on chance—I may not be able to make sense of every tragedy, particularly the apparently random ones. I may not have the knowledge or experience required to see cause-effect correlatives.

In relationships, however, I have plenty of proof, experience, and textbook advice that much of what happens to me is a result of my own choices. I believe when people genuinely examine their behavior and attempt to understand how they interact with others, forgiveness often comes into the picture.

I realized the right reasons weren't about blaming. I'd been through the anger; I didn't need to resurrect every tit for tat to understand why our relationship didn't work. More importantly for me was to understand how I contributed to a troubled and dying partnership. I had to review how I interacted, where the defenses came up, and why certain problems never resolved.

Understanding was the beginning of a much more exacting, yet exciting part of my journey. Unlike what some people might think, the party who chooses to leave a relationship feels the brunt of loss and confusion as well. Such a significant decision, laden with consequences, demands explanation. I'm not merely shrugging off my partner like an old coat.

Understanding is about learning. Understanding is about questioning. Observe children—little question-boxes whose survival hinges largely on learning why things are the way they are. How unfortunate, then, that I should pull up short of questioning one of the most important issues of survival, one concerning a companionship that so deeply impacts who I am and the way I live.

With time, I was able to more carefully consider where I had failed to act responsibly, or overmanaged, or simply followed my own interests at all costs.

Sometimes my best efforts in care giving (or actions I define as caring) don't fulfill the need. Sometimes the only loving thing left to do is to stop bailing my partner out of trouble. Sometimes it's impossible to rebuild a relationship on any other conjugal terms than co-dependency. And sometimes I have to stop taking responsibilities that are not mine, even at the risk of no longer being in control.

I later realized that my many misguided and unsuccessful attempts to manage aspects out of my control were making me a bitter, resentful person. With time, too, I was able to see a much larger picture at hand than simply a quick list of bad traits or faulty behavior. I was able to more fully understand how very important it is to give up some relationships.

Last Straws

When I first began listing my reasons for leaving, I automatically clicked off a page of last straws. For me, last straws were good for a chuckle or two, the surface material that divorces are made of, still far enough from the real reasons to avoid the pain. I think it's good to start with last straws while the hurt is too fresh for ferreting out the real reasons. You can jot them down on the back of your water bill, throw it in a drawer somewhere, and come back later for a good laugh (and a late charge).

Last straws are the stuff movies are made of. Have you noticed? In movies, people can do the impossible when it's the last straw. Dodge flying cleavers and meat hooks while delivering picture-perfect roundhouse kicks into the jaws of advancing galactic mutants (between screams). Open soup cans with nothing but bare molars. Steal one last lustful look at the damsel in distress while disabling a computer-coded booby trap . . .

Last straws are stranger than fiction, particularly when it comes to explaining our way out of a relationship.

"That's it! That's the last time he quits his job as a mall Santa!"

Now it occurred to me that, with our ever-advancing genetic research and DNA bio-engineering, we may soon see the day when you or I might inject our partner with whatever's lacking, the part that led us to the last straw in the first place. (Can you imagine the potentials here?)

We can rebuild her; we have the technology . . .

"I'm sorry, there must be some mistake. A typo, maybe? I ordered a DNA component that would make him slow in bed, not slow in the head." Or, "Jeez, do you think they mixed up my order? I got Madonna with a hangover, instead of a good time without the honey-dos."

Or perhaps all this DNA wizardry could have some real payoff after all . . .

"I'm sorry, li'l Johnny, but after your daddy's most recent DNA alteration, he can't say, let alone recognize, any four-letter words. The downside is, he can't help you with your spelling anymore, and you can't use any more four-letter words, either. The upside is, I can *shop* until I *drop!*"

Last straws are more fun than reasons because of their sheer absurdity. Reasons bring us back to the sobering truth, while last straws help us to kindly laugh at our biggest mistakes. And laughter, after all, is the best medicine for a broken heart.

By the next week, Quando was successfully adopted. His new owners, a couple with a generous love for their pets, kept Quando's widow apprised of his well-being with frequent visits until her death.

Della called me one day, a few weeks before she died.

"Do you see many like Quando?" she asked.

I could feel her hopefulness across miles of telephone line. "No," I finally said. "Not nearly enough."

"He was very special to me. Thank you for finding him a good home."

I tried to think of something to say. Nothing came.

"I still miss him sometimes, you know?" Her voice broke.

"I think—" I swallowed hard. "I think he understands."

I thought often about Quando as I searched for my own understanding. Particularly frustrating were dark days when sadness plunged me beyond reason, like Quando running circles in the recreation yard looking for his original master.

A Religious Question

One of the most difficult decisions was telling Sully that I thought our relationship was no longer in either of our best interests. I'd never concerned myself with moral or religious considerations about divorce because I'd never expected to divorce. As I turned to friends, family, and the church community, several well-meaning people challenged my decision. "God hates divorce," they said.

So do I. Divorce was not my first option, or consideration. Divorce was my last resort, as I believe it is for those of us who entered into our marriages caring about our spouses.

A possible condemnation from the Bible disturbed me. Does God condemn all divorce? I don't know. No one does. I do know that using religion to manipulate or control another person by infusing guilt or fear of punishment is one of the cruelest forms of exploitation.

I considered biblical references to divorce. Law under Mosaic regulation, written about 1406 B.C., speaks very specifically about the grounds for marital offenses in that culture. Under Levitical law, grounds for divorce lay at the sole discretion and possible error of the husband, and only he could issue a writ of divorce. Stipulations included intervention by a Levite priest to ensure legality, as well as appropriate grounds for divorce (something less than, but tending toward, adultery). Adultery itself was punishable by death in early Levitical law. *Some uncleanness* in later revisions became the catchall for shameful or offensive action fitting to raise reasonable jealousy or distrust in the husband's mind, thereby destroying any conjugal affection or harmony in the marriage. The death penalty was later dropped in the Mosaic law. A safeguard against the quickie divorce of the day provided that a man could not remarry a woman he had divorced.

Rather than justify this type of divorce, Christ admitted to its imperfection, both legislatively and morally. He pointed out its liability, particularly regarding the rights of women.

When the Pharisees—a religious sect intent on proving Christ as a fraud—questioned Him concerning this law, exception for adultery was still being made in the legal system in favor of the man. A man in that day might engage in polygamy or have multiple sex partners without being considered an adulterer.

This interrogation by the Pharisees in Matthew 19, a source of theological debate for centuries, has been used by clergy on both sides of the fence as a proclamation *for* and *against* divorce. Considering the nature of the law Christ was addressing, it's clear He was answering questions about a legal process that fundamentally and systematically excluded rights of women.

Given the opportunity for gross human error, I think Christ felt it necessary to remind these men about hypocrisy running deep within their own system.

Christ's is a much broader statement than at first meets the eye. Part of His goal was exposing religious hypocrisy of the day. Another part of His mission was redefining the law the Pharisees knew so well. What He says here about divorce is so much more than simply do or don't. Adultery works both ways from now on, Christ said. It's not just a man's prerogative and a woman's punishment. Furthermore, any revisions to laws concerning divorce should keep closer tabs on the potential abuses of the system.

Modern divorce law, while continuing to improve as a process, remains fraught with human error. It's highly unlikely that any legal system regarding such matters will ever operate successfully above the vicissitudes of human lust, inaccuracy, or injustice. Christ undoubtedly realized this.

While Jewish legislature lightened their punishment for the crime of adultery from death by stoning to scourging, and what amounted to divorce court, punishment by Greek and Roman law by comparison was far more severe—including banishment, heavy fines, mutilation, burning at the stake, and drowning.

Consider that without the changes in the penal system before Christ's birth, Joseph's only alternative by law, when faced with Mary's illegitimate pregnancy, was stoning. I believe Christ also took into account the options that the revised Jewish divorce laws offered His adoptive father—thereby sparing His mother—when He answered the Pharisees.

In contrast, the legal privileges available to women in this country today left me feeling all the more responsible. In a nutshell, I knew our difficulties better be irreconcilable. I had to be very sure there was no other way out or I would regret my decision. I had to carefully examine my reasons. Very carefully.

To understand my decision, I needed to examine the underlying nature of our relationship; what constituted its life, what led to its death. With time, I sorted through all those reasons. And with time, all the efforts that went into understanding why my first marriage failed comforted me in my loss.

CHAPTER 8
Acceptance

At our first meeting, Rosie stood confidently straining at the end of her leash. This was a dog my mother had spent months researching and preparing to acquire. Rosie was unremittingly proud, alert, and vigorous. Would she accept us? An important factor in adopting an older dog, I knew. At a time when I was struggling to embrace my own reality, Rosie came along, a twenty-pound blitzkrieg who demanded my undivided attention and acceptance.

Rosie

A solid black Scottie, Rosie was my parents' family companion for nearly four years. She'd washed out early in competitive dog shows and took great pains to prove herself not trainable (in lieu of participating in future shows, I think). Rosie had a lot of things figured out.

A robust and muscular rabble-rouser, Rosie was a handful of superior genetics and phobia of the moment. Many owners would've disliked her unpredictable moods.

Rosie's favorite pastime was snuffing out colonies of water bugs in the backyard. She'd come up from the hunt with a beard full of dirt, usually headed straight for her water bowl, then the couch.

Not much that happened around my parents' house went unnoticed by Rosie. She was quick to sound an alert concerning just about anything that moved. Her sharp barking became chronic background noise during most telephone conversations with my mother.

Rosie nearly intercepted the United Parcel Service truck on more than one occasion, and rarely tolerated another four-legged houseguest for long. She was likely to fiercely defend her territory at any given moment, and that territory was always subject to change.

My parents realized early on that they could neither train nor scold certain quirks out of Rosie; they were left to accept her on her own terms. My mother, especially, did this beautifully. They were a pair: Mother with her delicate, white skin, and Rosie, all bristly black.

One windy spring day I stopped by my parents' house, a little surprised by not meeting the ever-vigilant Scot at the door.

"Where's Rosie?" I glanced in the chaise lounge where she usually sat.

"With your daddy." Mother pointed out the window.

My father, on his four-wheeler, slowly turned at the corner of the house, heading away from us. I scanned the lawn for Rosie. Beyond the yard I saw no sign of that stubby black tail fording through the tall pasture grass.

Knowing Rosie's love for stalking anything on wheels, I cringed. "Are you sure that's a good idea?"

Outside, my father on the four-wheeler continued his slow trek around the driveway and through the yard.

As he changed course, I spotted Rosie, perched in front of him on the seat, nose high in the air.

"They go get the mail like that every day," Mother said, in all seriousness.

Unconditional Love

Rosie, it turns out, had a few pointers to teach us about acceptance. She died suddenly, without warning. She was just six years old. Pancreatic disease, an infirmity of some Scottish terriers, had killed her.

Rosie had exhibited early symptoms of pancreatitis and was treated with diet, medication, and exercise. Weight management, we'd learned, was an important component in treating this disease. No symptoms had recurred until the day of her death.

With Rosie's death, I found myself missing even the very doggie traits that irritated me most. I found this true, also, in the early days of my divorce. With the newness and starkness of being single again, I missed even the *unmissables*—like the dead-ended arguments about issues that only marginally affected our lives and never fully addressed the real problems. Had I made a mistake?

Accepting that our relationship was absolutely over was a door I'd erected over the threshold of resolving my loneliness, denial, and anger. I'd negotiated, bottomed out, and finally, finally understood. But I still had to walk through the door of acceptance. I had to accept that the relationship was, at last, really over. Then I had to shut the door.

Also, I had to begin to accept the man who'd once been my partner. With Rosie, our acceptance was about loving a dog on doggie terms. My acceptance of Sully was about realizing something new about unconditional love.

While I am sometimes called to love unconditionally, this doesn't mean that, in the normal course of life, I can continue to love without any conditions attached. A more obvious example is the restraint I exercise as a citizen every day. As a socially responsible adult, I will not likely tolerate for long what I believe to be illegal, immoral, or destructive behavior in my partner or in my child. This would not be beneficial to any party concerned or society as a whole. Therefore, if I want what is best for our relationship or family unit, I will love with conditions very much in place.

When I love unconditionally, I am accepting the circumstances and conditions I cannot change. Our relationship ended neither because I failed to love unconditionally, nor because I loved only with conditions. The relationship ended because I chose it to end.

I realized that my acceptance of my ex for who he was didn't mean I had to stay in that relationship and bear up with so-called unconditional love. That would be placing a condition on loving unconditionally, if you will. I've watched this—among other misconceptions about unconditional love—make many martyrs and destroy many lives.

In order to love unconditionally, sometimes two people must part ways. If a relationship has degenerated to a battle for changes that can't happen, this may be the only way to stop placing conditions on each other.

Loving unconditionally means that I accept Sully for who he is, while believing he will find his very best in life without me. Furthermore, this is the only way I can accept him for who he is. In this arena of acceptance, two people can wish each other well. Any follow-up conversation about an ex, therefore, is useless; it serves no purpose if my objective is to love unconditionally. For if I truly let go, I also relinquish any further attempts to control the unchangeable. If I continue to judge, I am continuing to actively evaluate. If I must judge anyone, it is far more productive if I judge myself.

If Only . . .

As I thought about the entire acceptance process, my thoughts naturally gravitated toward the unfulfilled "if onlys." I suppose we all have a few "if onlys" lurking around like broom handles in our closets. Like last straws, they are good for a few laughs. Life in general would look a whole lot different if only the fantasies that rode on those two little words somehow found their way into our paltry existence, would it not? Not necessarily better, mind you. Just different.

(Perhaps I should add, be careful what you wish for.) For how many times have I heard some version of the wishful thinking, "He could've had it all, if only his ship had come in"? What, exactly, does that mean? Really? We border on proposing these abstract concepts with all the dexterity of dipping fried squid.

I suppose that over time this poetic wishfulness has acquired the meaning that for lack of opportunity, or want of vision, or just pure and plain bad luck, the poor guy was prevented from coming into his own, right?

What, then, constitutes having it all?

"Joe Bob's a little down on his luck lately, huh?"

"Yeah, windfall taxes hit him pretty hard after winning the Lotto. But hey, he's still got that great broad, a Lamborghini, and all of his hair too."

"Yeah, man. He's got it all."

I'm glad we cleared that up. Now, what's this nonsense about his ship coming in? For the most part, nobody travels by ship on a routine basis anymore, do they? Could I be implying instead that he owns a ship? If that's the case, then what's the problem?

(On the Richter scale of worries, this trouble with a possibly sinking ship seems to measure out to more disastrous proportions than a purely personal matter, anyway. The *Titanic* and *Lusitania* come readily to mind.)

But I don't see many other possibilities, do you? Ah, now perhaps he's waiting at the wrong pier. A simple little mix-up at the travel agency.

This hardly seems fair, when this guy's entire future is riding on whether or not he's standing on the correct pier, waiting for his ship to come in. The arrival of this ship will determine if his hairline recedes. Not to mention the broad, the Lotto win, the Lamborghini, or the joy of dispensing his life's savings to the IRS.

I know, I know. Now I'm indebted to talk about—females. For this one, believe me, I searched far and wide (drum roll again, please).

"If only . . . she hadn't found herself between a rock and a hard place." Well, now. This does get interesting. I suppose about the only way she inexplicably found herself anywhere she didn't actually go was in the clutches of King Kong, or following one incredible bender. However she got there, I'm left fishing for the real explanation. Go ahead, tell your children it's like being grounded for life. Wherever she is, she's in so much trouble, she'll never want to find herself there again.

I could elaborate further about this rock and a hard place, but my ghastly little mind is already running away with that one. I think it's easier just to say she came out of a coma and found herself in some deep shit. Like the poor guy out there looking for his ship, she happened to be in the wrong place at the wrong time. Who knows, maybe while she was out there she even found his ship.

But unlike the guy, we'll never know what she's capable of doing or having if she does find her way out, because her "if only" is wedged between this rock and a hard place. (There you have it: sexual inequality still at work.) So she's sitting on an opportunity while he's still standing at the wrong pier.

Ah, the "if onlys." Is it any wonder why I struggle to accept my partner's imperfections?

Close Encounters

During her relatively short life, Rosie allowed only one person in our family to pet her. I'm not sure why, but perhaps somewhere in those early connections I made with Rosie, I simply refused to believe she disliked a rub now and then between the ears. That was a small part of her personality she changed for me, but no one else. I took great pride in being the only one who related to Rosie in this way. My privilege gave me a perspective about her that I thought no one else had.

But in the end, Rosie still struggled with the same health and disciplinary problems. My capability to associate with her in a relatively narrow part of her existence didn't guarantee anything in terms of her future or her fate.

So also in my first marriage, I learned that the capacity to relate to a spouse in a way nobody else can is not a good enough reason to continue a relationship. It's a great ego booster, and a romantic, short-term happy fix, but not enough in itself to carry the relationship forward.

With time, could Rosie have changed more? I'm not sure. I have great faith in capacity to grow: in myself, and in others. I know that "cannot" comes around far less frequently than "can." I also believe some of us find ways to love and accept our partners only by saying goodbye.

CHAPTER 9
Planning

I'm often amazed by the striking images the brain selectively retains. Many animals have their faces permanently etched on my memory. I can't explain, for instance, why I can recall a clearer picture of the wagging of a puppy's corkscrew tail, for instance, than a brilliant sunset in the mountains. One such memory that still gives me a hearty chuckle was my first chance upon a little lead-colored puppy that quickly earned the name Jughead. Courting a disaster of his own, Jughead reminded me of my own buffaloes as I planned for my life alone. The comedic nature of Jughead's predicament and the events surrounding his rescue echoed my own circumstances as I forged ahead.

JUGHEAD

Fattened on his mother's milk, this little mutt-hound I named Jughead dug under the fence and waddled off from the litter one day, about fifty yards down the county road cutoff. His curiosity nearly got the best of him.

The owners of eight husky little mountain dogs, including Jughead, lived just at the corner of the cutoff. When I drove by, I'd usually see the new arrivals trying each other on for size in the front yard, romping and wrestling in a pile on the ground, all seven black fuzz balls, except for Jughead. He was lead gray, and on that particular afternoon, he was out exploring the universe. In the nearest ditch, he'd found a soup can.

Or perhaps you might say it had found him.

As I turned the corner at the cutoff, I thought I'd just seen my first alien dog, or either a terribly deformed puppy. From the neck down, he looked like a regular pooch staggering around in the middle of the road. I was still about seventy-five yards away. The head though, looked like the end of a meat cleaver. Something wasn't right.

As I got closer, I realized this was one of the puppies from the corner house. The aluminum can stuck on his head matched his coat. He'd evidently gone for the goods in the bottom, ramming the can up past his ears. He had no idea where he was. He'd raise his muzzle to the sky, slam his head down on the ground after a fierce shake, then scrabble at the lip of the can with his forepaws.

I threw my car in park, jumped out, and ran down the middle of the road, flagging an oncoming car to a stop. Jughead heard me and, with the butt end of the can trained in my direction, waddled my way.

"Whoa, little fella." I scooped him off the road and waved a thanks to the motorist who kindly yielded to both of us. "How did this happen?"

When I first tried pulling the can straight out, nothing gave. I soon began wondering if I could get the can off. My panic level steadily rose. I feared Jughead would suffocate before I could successfully remove the tin; I also feared strangling him in the effort to remove it. Back at my car, I stroked the puppy's neck and back, trying to fight down fear and reassure him that the can removal was coming along nicely. Thankfully, the can was old enough that the edges were no longer sharp. It wouldn't budge; the lip was tightly wedged over his ears. I applied light leverage against his chest and tried a cautious twist. The can loosened, and with a little rocking motion, popped off.

Jughead blinked against the sunlight, still dazed by his time inside the can. I checked him for any visible injuries, finding—amazingly—none. His black baby's eyes were still taking the world in as a blur; I don't think he got much past the Aztec art design on my T-shirt. His belly was soft and round with all the benefits of adequate puppy fat. Although he had a streak of curiosity that would no doubt keep him in trouble, I could see that Jughead had a docile temperament. He was truly a keeper.

Putting on the Can

I didn't keep Jughead, though his owner made me a fast offer. She was soaking in the rays behind a push mower, the sun glancing off her metallic-orange bikini top.

"Wanna puppy?"

I stalled, dangling Jughead over the fence.

"Six weeks old today, first shots and wormed." I could see her fishing for a line to close the sale. "Looks like you, ya know?"

I slowly handed Jughead over, wishing I had room for him at home. But I didn't. "Don't they all," I said.

In his fix, Jughead reminded me of the early days of divorce, shortly after I'd accepted the reality I was starting over. Suddenly, an entirely different future loomed ahead of me. Emotionally, I was as blind as Jughead wearing a can, uncertain about my capabilities to cope with the daunting task of getting on with my life alone. It had been a while since I'd planned for one instead of two, and even longer since I'd entertained options purely of my own making.

Freedom?

Developing confidence in my capabilities to make informed, sound decisions without input from my ex was key to moving ahead with my future. I discovered my own resourcefulness and powers of analysis came quickly to my aid when I was forced to call upon them. I also realized that somewhere along the line, I'd begun to discredit their worth.

At first, I'd simply allowed Sully to tint my value judgments ever so slightly. Before long I seldom exercised my opinion anymore, because it seemed less of a hassle to accept the recommendations of my spouse, even if this meant his thinking for me. I put a can up around my ears just like Jughead, only mine was a voluntary laziness, if you will, or perhaps just hapless energy conservation for coexisting with all the things wrong that I couldn't make right.

Lobotomies

After talking with a significant number of women and men who experienced mind-numbing relationships, I gathered a consensus that might best describe the process as an elective frontal lobotomy. (Idiotic, you say. Nobody in his right mind elects for that kind of surgery.)

Precisely my point.

Now, here's where things get a little sticky though, in terms of exactly how or when I signed on the dotted line. I don't recall filling out any pre-op forms, though I must've done that much. I don't recall a precise date of surgery either. I think mine was more like leaving a tooth under my pillow for the tooth fairy, minus the fringe benefit of finding the quarter in the morning. I just woke up one day, looked in the mirror, and noticed a sizable cavity where my frontal lobe used to be. The lobotomy fairy strikes again!

Given my options, I must contend that's exactly the way it happened. That's the only way I can possibly explain how I lost the front quarter of my brain. (Oh, you say, but that makes my surgery non-elective. It must!) *If I can't even recall signing a form—*

Like I said, things get a little sticky here. How else can I explain why so many people must finally resort to that flimsy and worn-out excuse *I must've been totally out of my head?*

No, sir. No, ma'am—you, like me, were simply one of the many victims of the lobotomy fairy. A real no-brainer. (And yes, I'd like to know: When you signed on the dotted line, what were you thinking?)

At one time I thought about the alternative titles *Living with Your Lobotomy* or *Loving after Lobotomy,* but my editor suggested these bore too much explanation. After all, who wants to read about recovering from brain surgery, anyway? It's easy enough to commiserate with all the other lobotomy victims that I'm feeling, quite simply, ripped off. And by golly—it's time to go out and reclaim our brains and quarters and put them to good use!

Healthy Alliances

Not all alliances involve putting on the can. Appropriate reliance between partners can be beneficial to a relationship. I saw healthy love and trust existing around me every day. I wanted that.

Healthy reliance in a partnership gives me the freedom to express my most heartfelt value judgments and have them considered before challenged. It's a never-ending respect and thankfulness for my partner's differences, with an ever-present awareness that the world only as I see it is only through the eyes of one. The viewpoints of two can introduce a perfect check and balance into a relationship as long as both partners truly value and respect each other's differences.

But if I wear the can and choke out my own interests in deference to the concept of us, I'll soon see that the concept alone without a unified cooperation at work is just as hollow as the can that holds it. As surely as Jughead's encounter with the can could've cost him his life, so also does stuffing inside the can what I really like to feel and love to like, or my deepest intuitive value judgments. I wonder how many people every day share the life-stealing experience of wearing the can because they're convinced their opinions don't really matter. Is this living? Forcing on a mold of dishonesty about what I really feel and what I intuitively want will eventually hurt *us*.

When I first took off the can and began trusting my own judgment again, I didn't see a light at the end of the tunnel. I didn't really even see a clear path for a while. But with time, as my eyes adjusted, I found I could trust them to function normally again, to take me where I needed to go.

CHAPTER 10
Action

As months passed, the discourses with my animal guides, while assisting me in charting a steady course toward emotional recovery, remained unable to spare me the misery of night terrors. Intervening in my newfound balance and happiness, the nights brought on relentless fear. I would bolt upright in bed, clammy, seized with dread that I would surely go insane. If not for a wolf named Turbo who came out one night to greet me, I would've surely given in. He showed me simply where I needed to stop consigning pieces of my life away, that I had the power to choose and act upon those choices.

TURBO

Until I met Turbo, nightmares about incompleteness haunted me, about this unfinished business of leaving someone I'd loved.

Even in sleep there are few demons more startling than a mind divided against itself. The sense of awakening into the real world may not always bring relief. The emotional phantoms flanking furtively at my heels by day set out to mutilate me at night, exposing just how *instinctive* love can be. Then and now. In essence, my dreams were only infusing the past on the present—which nevertheless made my blood run cold.

Fear came to me at night because I was fighting my memories instead of facing them. Crickets stirring at dusk, a red August sunset, the smell of wood chips smoldering in a fire, everything in my day-to-day stream of consciousness triggered memories. Because I hadn't taken the time to examine my memories during my waking hours, they continued to haunt me at night.

A Nightmare

Several weeks after I met Turbo, I set out to identify his breed by his color pattern, that of the continental gray wolf. In my dreams, I'd lost my way inside an old abandoned house. Molded Sheetrock and tarpaper fell in on me as I wandered from one room to the next until the house finally allowed me a consultant of its choice. From the sticks of furniture, the rotten plank flooring, and the listing walls emerged the same shrouded form, room to room. Fifty or more phantoms stood motionless, as if programmed and awaiting some cue.

I could just make out their profiles, a man I've never seen, yet *knew*—each one the same.

I bolted. Outside, I scrabbled for a foothold, darting this way and that. Trees took root all around me. I stumbled over them as they shot up just inches in front of my face. I clawed my way through the undergrowth, my speed giving way.

Turbo leapt out of the underbrush. It never occurred to me to be frightened of him, this wild ancestor of dogs. He knew these woods. He would show me the road to safety. Turbo came out to meet me head-on, at the last moment paring away to my right.

On impulse, I turned the opposite direction. I know the dangers of turning one's back to an animal: I have a bite scar to prove it. But Turbo was no ordinary animal. I peeled away to the left.

Going left is symbolic of choosing intuitively. Through hard knocks, I've come to have a greater respect for powers of intuition. I've learned that the guidance of gut feelings is not so much from the gut as the vernacular implies, for as we reach adulthood, we've selectively developed a summary of our experience in order to survive. That summary is, for the most part, intuition.

I knew that Turbo wouldn't give chase. He was acting as a decoy for me, one I'm certain the phantoms will never overtake. For I could see already how he'd arrived before me, resolute in his purpose and majestic in his journey.

I made it my resolve to examine my dreams long enough to push past the terror and hear the heartbeat. Most of my dreams were about unresolved elements in my past—scattered peppercorns of pain, tiny smells, hints of goose flesh, or flashes of time and place—a stirring of things remembered that tugged at my deepest insecurities, my greatest guilt, and my meanest failures.

Sometimes separation doesn't afford us opportunities to physically return and re-experience all of our past. But I knew I could return to some of mine, even if only in thought. Revisiting the places of my past in my new single state was helpful for purging old ghosts. By setting up new memories, I reaffirmed my decision to take action and move forward. I confirmed to myself that I refused to live in the past—in its glory, or its failures.

So my recovery at this point became about taking action. Some days required pure grit to rise up out of my own emotional cesspool and plan a day's schedule. Grief tempted me to drift, to leave life to chance. My decision for recovery prompted me to reconnect with family and friends, to draw upon their strength as needed. Though in some ways this proved difficult for me, I knew I would ultimately be more capable to return their kindness if I learned to accept their help. Being around people I cared about was essential to my healing.

The rest was up to me: caring for myself with adequate nourishment, rest, exercise, and medical attention; making mental steps to expand my spirit, intellect, and individual empowerment; daring to dream, and daring to make my dreams come true.

Operation Flush

I have a wonderful friend who doesn't let me get by with much. He measures his solid, eighteen-inch biceps three times a week and freaks out at the thought of eating a baked potato loaded.

"Hold it right there," he said. "That's all real sappy about the pooch and the sandman, but now that I'm divorced, I could swear I just checked out of hell. We're talking Waco, man. What do you mean, go back?"

I had to think about this. After contacting my military consultant and my editor, I agreed that, unfortunately, some memories are much like land mines. No way around them, no how.

"A highly volatile situation, ma'am. Wouldn't go back there if I were you."

Okay, so—let's say I can't go back. Impossible. Something would explode. I've still got to purge the demons, right?

According to the military expert, my situation could become potentially hostile. This is definitely a job, he says, for a strategic, front-line maneuver called Operation Flush.

Here's how it works: any potentially hostile or incendiary devices go into this gigantic titanium toilet. This, by the way, is the Mother Of All Toilets. It's bullet-deflecting, fireproof, and detonation resistant. *Pile 'em high, boys!* Now I can simply flush all my hard luck away, no matter how particularly insidious or combustible it might be. Who needs nostalgia? Back into the landfill my troubles go, carried away by the ingenious Operation Flush, along with the rest of the cockroaches in my life.

"So there," I say. "You, too, can take your relic and flush it."

My potato-eating friend liked the idea.

Don't you feel better already?

Yes, I finally had to agree that there are indeed some places to which I don't want to return. For those memories, a little laughter can go a long way into making a truly (and yes, pun intended) satisfying cathartic experience.

Old Haunts

Some demons are tough to drive out. A few of mine existed long before they became part of my relationship. Some haunts in my past I cannot change. What I can change is my resolve to leave them there in my past, bear what consequences may remain, and explore new heights of life ahead.

Turbo, my helper of the night, is the constant cadence of man's best friend taking on parts of the soul he cannot lay to rest. Turbo encourages me to take up the remainder of my soul—the one that maintains life, health, and vitality—and charge ahead. I suppose many of us have seen Turbo at least once, if only the flash of his tail over a midnight horizon, outrunning the killing hounds.

CHAPTER 11
Forgiveness

On the difficult days, fresh air and exercise went a long way for preserving my sense of wholeness. During jogs around my parents' country homestead, I'd frequently pick up a neighborhood stray or two—unleashed, loose dogs that would run the loop with me to hang out on the porch for a while, then make their way back home. Carly was one, and she came along on such a day when forgiving my ex proved particularly demanding.

Carly

Carly, with her rich chocolate coat, was a husky Labrador who navigated on three legs. A true survivor, Carly had lost her front right leg up to the withers in a hunting accident. She'd also whelped several litters, even recently. Her teats hung like pouches, floppy and worn from overuse.

I could see right away that life would've been much easier for Carly if she'd lost a hindquarter instead. As it was, the trauma to her spine was profound, heaving her backbone into a camel's hump, gnarled and listing toward her missing limb. Her withers pinched together, arthritic already from her efforts to support half her body on one front leg, bowed and canted like a wheel hitching away from its axle.

What amazed me about Carly was her undaunted effort to run right alongside me with a hobbling and seemingly untiring gait. She was painful to watch. Here was Carly, a dog I guessed to be barely six, having lost her leg in a gambit play on a hunting field and traded down to a local bitching mill, running free and unencumbered by all the bitterness life had offered her. In her luminescent, sterling eyes I saw only forgiveness.

Carly harbored no bitterness, and, remarkably oblivious to her handicap, remained busy doing the things she loved: running, retrieving, and frequenting water holes. She'd flush out a covey of quail, then trounce into the nearest gulch, icicles clinging to her belly. Wherever Carly went, she carried forgiveness with her—which remains her lightest of loads.

Considering a Pardon

I still see Carly now and then when I visit my parents, and her resilience always amazes me. Her owners have since stopped breeding her, but she continues to wear the scars of multiple litters and degenerative arthritis. She runs with me on the good days, as playful and hopeful for a quarry in the reeds as she ever was.

I place Carly at the end of Part I, because for me, forgiveness came last. Forgiveness was tough.

Forgiveness by nature is complex, a stage I thought I'd reached long before I truly got there. While anger and hurt still bubbled up in my thoughts concerning my ex, I knew I hadn't forgiven.

I knew I couldn't sidestep forgiveness either. If I did, I simply wouldn't heal.

In its complexity, however, forgiveness often must be cultivated. Sometimes an offender can be forgiven while the offense cannot. If I can forgive both, I am the better for it. But in remaining congruent with my value systems concerning illegal, immoral, or self-centered behavior, I realized forgiving an offense might not always be possible. I don't think we can expect someone who has been wronged or violated in a truly evil way to embrace evil and maintain any semblance of self-respect. I believe some people have the right to hold onto the truth that they have been violated. Others may find it possible to hate the evil that impacts their lives while forgiving their offenders.

This isn't easy. It wasn't easy for me. It's only natural, I think, to measure the degree of forgiveness to the degree of the offense. But healing became more important to me than maintaining my hurt and anger, whether toward my ex or toward myself.

Forgiving myself also became part of the equation. In some ways, forgiving the self is more difficult. I had to come back around to accepting the elements of choice that still existed, even in what seemed to be my purest of emotional responses. I realized that even working through my feelings involved elements of choice.

And choice is empowering.

I could choose to forgive my ex.

I could choose to forgive myself.

I'd already decided, for example (after resolving the relationship was finished, and that this was for the best), that I would learn to assert positive thoughts about myself. For me, forgiveness came after my starting over began taking me to better places. The choice to forgive became easier after choosing to make my life a positive, safe place and taking action to do and be my best.

The offenses and struggles of the past forced me to a higher place I had heretofore only dreamed of going. I could've circumvented the pain of leaving, of course, by staying—and missed the many blessings that lay ahead. One of those blessings was forgiveness. For the short-term, it would've been easier for me to remain in a relationship that was wrong and to remain the bitter, angry person I was.

Now I'm glad I didn't.

Retro Gum

Simple concept: a mood-altering gum. A real hit at parties. I'll call it Retro Gum. Retro Gum, not to be confused with retrospect or retrograde, is the pharmaceutical solution for forgiveness. If I pop a piece, I simply short-circuit that one fraction of a millimeter along a dendrite that so painfully remembers how I was wronged, snubbed, *dissed.* You get the picture. So with this gum I can go into retro—before my pain—at least until the flavor wears out.

Ever noticed how little children, kittens, puppies—babies in general—live largely in the present? If I don't give the little tyke the cookie before supper *now*—well, according to him, I may have just committed the biggest crime in all history. As I withhold the cookie in one hand, read my toddler disciplinary manual in the other, and listen to screams, lo—I read that children before age five have virtually little understanding of time or consequence. So if I withhold the cookie until after supper, what is twenty minutes to me means forever to him. Until he can grasp language and other skills necessary to understand I'm not holding out on him *forever*, he'll continue to scream his way through life. Thank Mother Nature, therefore, for the power of distraction. If I turn him in a different direction and offer him a shiny red balloon, he may very well forget about the cookie and my offense—possibly indefinitely.

Now, I suppose that a truly successful Retro Gum would re-create some of this seamlessness we experience as children. Possible side effects: forgetfulness, thumb-sucking, and screaming.

If Retro Gum became a real household item, some of our lingo would definitely change. "Has she forgiven you yet?"

"Not sure. But she's been in Retro for five hours now."

Corporations would probably construct Retro Lounges, though I can't say a retro break would totally replace the need for a cappuccino or a smoke. Retro bars and grills? Hmm . . .

I suppose, too, that Retro Gum would probably soon find its way into a transdermal patch, though sustained-release forgiveness wouldn't be nearly as interesting, I think.

So—should Retro Gum or any other comparable mind jammer find its way into my local pharmacy, you bet I'd be curious. I'm not sure I'd want any retro experiences myself, but I'd be interested in hearing some personal success stories!

Bitter Potential

As I talked with others in recovery, I saw that for many, an unforgiving attitude can be the last protective stronghold to dismantle. Forgiveness takes time.

The tremendous reserves I could expend on anger, revenge, or reliving personal affronts are far better spent on energizing, positive assertions as I choose to forgive myself and my ex, and go on with my life.

Forgiveness is like airline baggage. As I stand at the baggage claim, I'm going to identify my own baggage and take it with me. My bags are all I can handle right now. I own up to them, that they gave my former relationship a load of trouble. I forgive myself for having them still. I leave my ex's baggage on the claim belt. That's his stuff. If I don't carry it around anymore, then I have no reason to be weary or angry. I don't confuse his problems with mine anymore. That's forgiveness.

Forgiving is tough. I think my attorney, who, after handling hundreds of divorce settlements, summed it up best when he said, "People go in unhappy and they come out unhappy."

While our legal system does better than most in determining fair allocations of alimony, child support, custody, visitation rights, and property division—no divorce is perfect, and most, anything but amicable. Human greed, retaliation, and sense of entitlement too often come into play.

I'm always wary of people who talk about cordial divorces and how everything's forgiven for the sake of the children or social reasons or whatever. Sure, if I come out of a divorce settlement getting everything I want, I might feel everything's just peachy too. But that's not forgiveness.

Herein lies the quandary: divorce, no matter how overtly friendly, grows out of betrayal. Divorces can have accompanying legal and financial obligations for many years. Maybe I am left alone to forgive my ex without his knowledge, then move forward with my life. I'm left with good and bad memories I choose to lay to rest so that I can forgive.

But what if I face daily consequences of a divorce settlement for years on end? Does forgiveness come when the last alimony dollar is paid, or when the children turn eighteen? Can I rise above even these circumstances with a forgiveness that stands apart from my hurt (or my wallet), because I know that if I continue to carry a grudge, I only continue to carry my ex with me?

If I find myself needing to forgive aside from strident circumstances, I hold no illusions. That kind of forgiveness is tough.

I need to forgive like Carly.

I need to forgive from my heart.

Carly remains my constant teacher of how very important forgiveness can be. For in a world where any good or evil is possible, the greatest risk I can take is becoming a victim of my own unforgiving spirit.

"I once had a sparrow alight upon my shoulder for a moment while I was hoeing in a village garden, and I felt that I was more distinguished by that circumstance than I should have been by any epaulet I could have worn."

—Henry David Thoreau

Part II

Intimacy

CHAPTER 1
Attraction

Heartwarming as well as heartbreaking, my experience volunteering for the animal shelter offered many poignant moments. A young, healthy animal bouncing around in an animal crate with fresh water, food, and toys was always a welcome sight. These were the animals that attracted adoptions and new owners who reassured me I made a difference at the shelter—for an hour, a day, or a lifetime.

The process of adopting a new pet or developing a new interpersonal relationship involves establishing unfamiliar bonds and boundaries that can be both exhilarating and frightening. After staggering through the grieving process, I thought I was content to spend some time in limbo. *Flux* was becoming a comfortable concept.

But there he was. Another man. A new relationship. Was I ready? Was he?

ESMERALDA

Esmeralda, an eight-week-old kitten with calico markings, spent half her day diving under the newspapers that lined her cage and the other half scaling its bars. She went along upside down, if that suited her purposes. Esmeralda was both perplexed and intrigued by her surroundings. The identification card that hung on the door got a merciless, sporadic pummeling whenever convenient—over and under and through the bars.

Inside her cage, Esmeralda reminded me of all that is spontaneous and raging—but most of all, alive. To me, to remain alive and in love means sharing both the fascinations and frustrations of companionship—every day for a lifetime.

Yet Esmeralda outside of her cage was not the little terror I'd expected. The multicolored streak became docile as a baby when she was outside, and eager to be petted. The only object worthy of exploration in the room was the lavatory drain, which is an old cat custom.

Most of us have experienced the tiny laughter that bubbles up in new love, the awkward moments as well as the personal asides we remember, sometimes beyond everything else. The capacity to experience new love, I believe, is something we never outgrow. In all of those moments I see Esmeralda, a baby so caught up with romping and living and being, she hasn't yet considered anything more, or less.

A Surprise

I'd found new love again. Was it possible? Was it wrong? These questions tumbled over each other in my mind the moment I saw him walk around the corner of Faye's house. He wore what was obviously a favorite (and ragtag) pair of sweats. I had a terrible cold and was toting a box of Kleenex. You might say neither one of us was on our best foot. Before I'd fully registered what was happening, we were being introduced.

"Julie, meet Jim." Faye gave me a guileless smile and returned to blowing leaves off her porch. Hansel, satisfied it was only me, set off around the corner of the house after another dog I didn't recognize. *Was this a setup?*

I looked at Faye, then back at Jim. He did have a nice smile. *Nah, Faye wouldn't.* The questions continued jousting each other in my head. *Was a nice fellow like Jim supposed to come into my life this early? This late? Now?*

In this journey into new love after our relationship losses, I knew Jim and I owed it to ourselves to approach this new relationship at a comfortable pace, with equal amounts of passion and caution. For me, fully accepting and understanding my former relationship paved a foundation of confidence for choosing Jim to be my next mate. I could make positive choices with positive outcomes. I didn't have to make the same mistakes twice. I had learned some valuable lessons from my previous experience. Positive affirmations like these were all an outgrowth of acceptance, understanding, and forgiveness.

With that much said, I knew I still needed to approach this relationship differently. I wanted and needed an unwavering commitment on the front end. I needed several components that were missing in my prior relationship. Jim did, too. (If you boil it down, I guess you could say we both knew what we didn't want.)

Though I still had trouble believing this turn of fate, I'd just been introduced to someone who met all of those needs without the asking. It seemed too good to be true.

My first instinct was to be prepared to politely but cautiously back away. Old hurts were still too fresh.

Friends and family were warning me to move ahead slowly. I tried to listen equally with my head and my heart. As this new relationship with Jim developed, I realized how easy it would be to put up defenses and hold against him what happened with Sully. How natural it was to superimpose the past on the present for fear of making the same mistake! I imagined I could see a tiny similarity here, a germination of a habit there, or an inconsistency that would surely mushroom into the same unpleasant experience I'd had before. Was he feeling this way too? We talked about it.

Sure, we were frightened—frightened of repeating the past. After all, it's only human to cling to what's familiar, even at the expense of our own well-being. Yes, we were capable of repeating our mistakes. Did we have the inner resources to regroup and move into a new relationship for some totally different reasons this time? Would these reasons make the difference whether we stayed together happily?

Key to answering many of those perplexing questions that popped up early in our relationship was understanding what we were experiencing: the fascination and frustration of starting over. We had six more stages of intimacy ahead of us. Some of our questions were simply impossible to answer at that time. So we saved them for later.

In a healthy, happy, and promising relationship, what makes the difference? If I could bottle up this mysterious ingredient, I'd be the wealthiest woman in history. Is it personality? Compatibility? Maturity?

Early in our relationship, Jim said, "Funny—I don't even know your birthday, but I know your heart." Of course, he didn't know all of my personal habits and idiosyncrasies. He didn't know everything that had happened to me since I was two. But he understood the driving force. He was saying he could clearly see what motivated my thoughts and actions. Like it or not, a person's driving force can outlast a relationship. What drives me every day—what I search and yearn for most—determines how I connect my life to Jim's.

In our new relationship, Jim and I soon realized that neither one of us had to prove ourselves better than our previous mates. We didn't need to play comparison games. No need to compete. Simply knowing more about our individual wants, needs, and limitations in this relationship was all that really mattered.

Esmeralda somersaulted all around us. Cartwheels and double-gainers. Colors were brighter. Food was richer.

I enjoyed this passionate *starting over* as much as I continue to enjoy our attraction every day I awaken. Over time a single question kept coming up, and it served as a barometer or rating scale of our new relationship: *How does it feel to wake up beside my mate today? Cozy? Overworked? Unchallenged? Contented? Bittersweet?*

I carried forward lessons from my past, left old battles behind, and entered this new attraction with Jim for different reasons than my first marriage. After fueling up with optimism, I stared a new reality square in the face and relinquished battles that no longer mattered. We were starting over, together. A new horizon. This was great!

Jim attracted me with different personal qualities than had attracted me in my first marriage. Kindness over boldness, for example. Certain character traits became more important to me the second time around because I fully understood their necessity in a long-term, loving relationship.

With every personal asset comes its weakness when it is overextended or called upon with selfish intentions. Boldness becomes a daredevil, or an indiscriminant public display. Kindness becomes a pushover, or brown-nosing. Tenacity becomes relentless pursuit, overbearing, or tiresome. Under the stress of overextending, I realized I could very possibly begin hating the qualities that once attracted me. *So that's how love turns to hate!*

I had to turn the mirror on myself. What about those personal assets and quirks of mine that had initially attracted Jim? I found that keeping attractions attractive requires the same kind of ruthless self-examination and honesty I was forced to call upon in my journey through grief. It's not always pleasant when I have to ask myself: Where do I overextend? The second time around, Jim and I have a much better grasp concerning what attracts for the long term, and how much of the good stuff we can give or take before too much of the good stuff becomes bad.

Chemistry

Some circles of anthropology and biology have published marvelous, enlightening documentation on the urge called *lust*—a hankering for those physical features and personal mannerisms that attract—and why, at times, the pickings seem so slim. First of all, some say, I have to come to grips with the so-called *primitive* section of my brain, and that, yes, I actually use it. Circulating around in these little clusters of gray matter are packs of horny genes, like scrubbing enzymes in tub cleaner. There my hormones are, ready to wreak havoc on my life, having me apt to hop in the sack just when I least expected.

Some scientists call it the *mating urge.* Survival of the species. It's the drive to pick a healthy-looking sex partner with good genes and carry on. Make more beautiful kids. My friend, Faye, would like someone with most of his teeth.

But—do you or I *really* want healthy children or a good time? The boundaries get a little fuzzy here. After all, we're looking at chemicals, right? A reptilian brain. Very primitive stuff, you see. (So go ahead and look for a mate with two ears that match, and when you find that person who absolutely sets you on fire—try not to forget why it's called "chemistry.")

Keeping Esmeralda

Esmeralda double-flipped her way out of the shelter into a nice family, a Noah's Ark concept favoring multiple mixed adoptions, both man and beast. Her total time spent at the shelter was about two weeks, during which we named her our "Ragin' Cajun." Esmeralda's new owners gave their reason for adopting her as simply, "We were completely taken with her."

CHAPTER 2
Friendship

I hadn't been divorced long—not time enough to engage in any long-term dating, or, for that matter, dating at all. I was prepared to embark on the standard two years of divorce recovery, with any forthcoming relationships to develop at a snail's pace—and certainly not intending to defy those bounds.

I was also terrified of the "transition" relationship I'd heard about—the head-over-heels love affair that often follows a divorce—born out of a need to escape loneliness, guilt, and pain. As I remember it, I was just again becoming comfortable in my own skin when I met a shelty named Buck. I was about to learn how to be a friend.

Buck

I never knew Buck as a puppy. Only pictures. I would like to have known Buck and his master, Jim, much earlier, but they both came into my life later, when I was fully ready to experience their friendship.

Buck, a strapping, seven-year-old shelty, was curious about who'd come to visit. As he bolted around the corner of the house with Hansel that first Sunday in November, I had no idea I was being subjected to an interview—by a dog. Buck was evaluating my friendship quotient. That's the best way to describe our first encounter. At the same time Buck—not just Faye—introduced me to his master, Jim, who would soon become my second mate.

As Buck looked up at me with those responsive brown eyes, I imagined he might be thinking, *Here, let's check this out. After all, it's me you'll have to contend with for the rest of your life. That guy back there, he's just along for the ride.*

Buck and I came to terms early in our relationship with the daily grooming. I learned to be very careful not to yank through the undercoat. It brought me great satisfaction to see Buck begin to enjoy this time, belly exposed, head lolled to one side. A typical shelty, Buck needed to be treated with tenderness.

I didn't realize it at the time, but so did I. Buck brought someone I'd been wanting to know all my life. Such compassion became the theme of our relationship: much tenderness need be applied.

Who's a Friend?

Buck began our friendship using all his senses, sniffing me over, eyeing the hand that came out of my coat palm up, circling me a couple of times in a neurotic, herding fashion. For Buck, meeting me was all about discovery—whether I had food, if I'd had food in the last twenty-four hours, if food might become a priority for me in the near future. I say this not to disparage Buck for his appetite, but as an example of his first focus. He would form other opinions later about whether I was generally kind, or if he would become an object of my affection. He would challenge my authority to see just how far he could push the envelope. But his first focus was about what he wanted and needed most.

First focus in my newfound friendship with my second mate was all about discovery, wants, and needs too—but with distinct divergence from the first time around.

I realized that friendship means different things to different people—even my mate.

What is a friendship? A weekend golfing buddy? A childhood school chum? A yearly Christmas card? The only person in the world who understands exactly how you feel? A multi-level marketing opportunity? A person who keeps damaging information about you in complete confidence? Someone you thought would never betray you? Or is a friend, as Christ has said, *with no greater love than this, one who will lay down his life for his friends?*

It's reasonable to assert there are many levels of friendship. In the deeper stages of intimacy, the nature of friendship changes. Some might even measure friendship quotient by what's at stake. I am a different friend to a roommate versus a houseguest, and different still to a family member.

I think good friendships help us stretch our personal boundaries. My friendship with Jim has challenged me to give what I thought I didn't have, to reach goals I doubted I could attain, and to alter personal standards that only served to prevent me from being my best.

The second time around, I sought to become a better friend. I sought to become less intrusive with my communication. I sought to be a better communicator—

by listening first to Jim's complete thoughts without finishing them for him.

A counselor once told me that most adults become masters at finishing sentences, especially around those they love. Because I know my parents, spouse, or child so well, I generally know how they think and feel. I can usually predict what they may do or say. When conversations turn to difficult subjects and I see Jim struggle to find the right words, it's all too easy to try to help him out, to finish his sentences. Even if I don't say anything, my brain has more than likely already filled in the blanks. I've heard what I thought he was saying without really hearing what he actually said. I've superimposed my thoughts over his. I've intruded.

I also realized that keeping a friendship on a more intimate level is about making mistakes—even those habitual errors resulting more from personal flaw than fluke—from negligence, impulsiveness, greed, or discontentment. I had to level with the fact that both Jim and I will keep making mistakes as long as we live. It's called human nature. But I also learned that when mistakes are made, it's far less painful and harmful to our friendship to openly admit them, assume responsibility for them, and, in that way, minimize the damage.

Verbal Abuse

One of the toughest behaviors to break (and, incidentally, one of the most damaging) is verbal abuse. Verbal abuse is simply an attempt to belittle, manipulate, or pass the buck with words. If I *crack wise* with my friends using put-downs and sarcasm, is it all only in good fun?

Or is it, starting even as early as in adolescence, a germination of verbal and physical abuse?

If this sounds like a far cry, consult the nearest battered women's shelter. A collective opinion from counselors who know and see results of abuse every day is that an abusive relationship is a 99 percent closed situation. In other words, the chances of an abusive partner even becoming aware of the problem is next to nil, and the chances of stopping the behavior permanently are even less. The emotional roots of abuse are anger, fear, and insecurity. An abuser means damaged goods—sometimes long before the victim stumbles into the equation.

At the heart of an insult, no matter how seemingly benign, is condescension, criticism, and hate. Couching these attitudes inside jokes doesn't make them any less harmful.

Over the long haul, my friendships are only as good as the friend I'm willing to be, which includes what I do and don't say. Thoughtfulness, sensitivity, and tenderness are key ingredients to good and long-lasting friendships.

A Friend in Need

I married Buck's master, Jim, and had known both of them about two years when our friendship was put to the acid test. With the snap of mid-February in the air, Buck was out roaming the pasture. I was reaching for a white windbreaker that would zip over eight-and-a-half months of pregnancy when the telephone rang.

At the other end, a frantic neighbor told me she'd just seen Buck attacked by a stray dog at the end of our property.

"Had him down by the throat and mauled him good before I could get out there," she said. "Buck got up and ran off, back toward your place."

I thanked her, hung up, grabbed my car keys, and headed for the front of the house. I knew Buck. He'd stand his ground in a fight. He'd never retreat unless the situation was really bad. Through the window I saw him.

Buck stood at the front door, his head cocked at an odd angle, swaying. His mane, predominantly white, was now red. Behind him I saw a thin trail of blood on the porch.

I threw off my Windbreaker and grabbed a towel in one motion, running for the door. The glazed-over stare I got as I wrapped the towel around him confirmed that Buck was going into shock. He sank into my arms.

Buck weighs more than forty-five pounds. But for the next hour, he was light as a feather. I was on adrenaline-charged autopilot. Didn't feel a thing. I parked him on top of the ledge that I called my belly at that time and off we went.

I'd vaguely remembered my neighbor informing me that she'd called ahead to the veterinarian's—a good turn that spared me the time and frustration of doing so. We roared our way through town, flashers going, speeding over the limit as fast as I dared. Buck lay very still in the passenger's seat, breathing rapidly. *I had to get there soon.* The message replayed in my head as I dodged around drivers, most paying no attention to the sport-utility vehicle on their bumpers with neon-orange lights flashing in their rearview mirrors.

At the veterinarian's, the assistant met me at the door. She is a slender woman who handles both the front desk and the kennels in this small office with a rapid efficiency. "Oh, my goodness." Her face fell. "We got a call that you were bringing in a dog—but not a wounded dog," she said. "The doctor's just left for a farm call, way out in the woods. There's no way I can reach him."

The vet would be out there at least a couple of hours, she said. We both looked down at Buck, lying on the examination table. His breathing was very shallow. The only other veterinarian nearby was a horse vet. So I called Jim and broke the news.

"Bring him to my office," Jim said. "I'm no vet, but I think I've got what we need here."

A physician in private family practice, Jim is very cautious about using his medical skills on animals. He'd explained before that while some carryovers exist, administering sedatives and surgical procedures on animals can be tricky.

Buck and I sped to the opposite side of town, to Jim's office. Buck was, thankfully, not bleeding anymore.

In the surgical room, we washed down the examination table and got to work.

"I want to make sure we irrigate the wound real well," Jim said. He began pouring sterile saline solution over the general area while I trimmed away hair.

I stopped. “Will this cause more bleeding?” I asked. “Because I don’t think he can stand to lose much more.”

Jim tore open a sterile suture kit. I could tell by the way he laid out his instruments that he didn’t want to answer. “We’ll see.” By parting and trimming the hair, we soon found a one-inch diameter hole in Buck’s throat. It flared open just to the right of his trachea, bleeding lightly.

Jim tipped the surgical light to look. “That’s good,” he said.

I stepped away from the table, feeling sick. Tried to concentrate on breathing. “Wha—” The baby kicked me in the ribs. “What’s good?”

“No damage to the trachea or the esophagus,” he said, flushing more saline down the hole. He anesthetized the area with Emla cream and looked at me. “Maybe you should sit down.”

Eight sutures later, Buck was declared stable enough to go home. Jim slept that night on the floor beside him. Through the night, we rotated turns on the hour giving Buck water through a food syringe.

The next day, Buck tried to stand, but couldn’t. We repeated the syringe every hour with sugar water and finally got him to nibble on soft dog biscuits.

Buck couldn’t bark for a week. He moped around the house and lay quietly at my feet. I missed him terribly—the feisty old Buck who sounded an alarm about anything real or imaginary that moved across the perimeters of our property. I took him to the vet for a follow-up, medication, and orders to rest.

By the following week, Buck had regained most of his voice, and much of the swelling was gone. Before long he was moving freely about, romping and herding the world around him as before. What had changed, though, was our experience of friendship. Buck now knows I am truly there for him, as he is for me. We both have a far better understanding about just how much we need each other.

Nursery Rhyme Friends

Three weeks later our son was born. As months passed, baby gifts of every size and shape, plus many stuffed animals and toys, crowded into our house. We soon had several tapes of nursery rhyme songs, a talking car phone, and other interactive toys that have been playing loudly for the duration of writing this book. A friend of mine wisely pointed out that some of these songs also play in hell—after hearing them for hours and days and months and years on end.

One tune that is well barbecued in my brain already is a cute little song about friendship:

> Be kind to your web-footed friends,
> For that duck may be somebody's mother.
> Be kind to your friends in the swamp,
> Where the weather is cold and damp!

When the song reaches the part about you may think that this is the end, I'm glad it is!

So one of the first songs many of us hear as children is already trailblazing respect for friends lower in the food chain. The song also promotes the survival of the species (that primitive brain again) and watching out for pals in need, or those a little under the weather. I'm amazed how much ground this simple tune covers as it introduces several levels of friendship.

Historically speaking, I think we can measure the general kindness of any society by the way its adults treat its animals and its children, with the trickle-down effect of how its children treat its animals. Be kind to your web-footed friends. If we can learn this much about friendship before we are two, why stop there?

Treading Tenderly

Today Buck extends his friendship to many children with cerebral palsy during our pet therapy visits at a nearby rehabilitation center. He lies quietly and unafraid on a therapy table while these crippled children struggle to brush him. He is content to extend himself here because he knows in the end he'll come out well groomed and well fed.

Buck regularly reminds me that good friendships often tread tenderly. Life is tough enough. I bring all my hurts with me, and some wounds run deeper than soul or skill can see. I must rally my mate—my best friend—as my ally, and have the patience to let real companionship over time do its tender work.

CHAPTER 3
Foundations

Sydne, a tiny Chihuahua puppy, was just discovering life and the great big universe around her when my own world came crashing down around me with the loss of my first marriage. Sydne demonstrated early to me that the foundations for a healthy relationship begin with attitude. I was grateful then for her companionship, as I am still. I'm thankful, too, for Sydne's joy and love of life, the spunky little spirit who dutifully earned her nickname "the tiny giant."

Sydne

Sydne, an apple-headed Chihuahua, was born on a stormy night in early April. She loved thunderstorms. For her, life was one big bolt after the other, and she was determined to stretch it to its limits. At her six-weeks' checkup, Sydne weighed three ounces. Three pounds later she was fully grown, and a very weighty part of my existence.

I never saw Sydne reach her wit's end about anything, not even during a series of surgeries and treatments for several congenital birth defects her first year. Life gave her a rough start with the often incurable demodectic (red) mange and a medial-luxating (hypermobile) kneecap. By the time she was eight months old, she'd been through three surgeries.

But Sydne had an amazing ability to bounce back enough to keep her bouncing for years to come. I ran her patience dry with forty minutes' daily rehabilitation for her knee, dog-paddling in five inches of bathtub water.

A cinch, it wasn't.

Sydne's first "swim" was more like a three-pound tsunami. Try as I might to gently lower her in, she squirmed out of my grip and scrabbled up the side of the bathtub.

"Not so fast," I'd say, and put her back in. We repeated this several times before she settled into walking along the shallow end of the tub with a chuff. That was one wet, mad Chihuahua.

Sydne soon discovered that the wetter I was, the less total swimming time she got. We made a few compromises along the way, however, and somehow got through it. And she never failed to rapidly regain composure for her reward—the double stuffing of Oreo cookies.

Sydne grew out a healthy coat of fawn-colored fur and manages well with her bum knee, stabilized by a titanium pin the diameter of a sewing needle. The key to her amazing recovery, besides a terribly doting owner, was simply her attitude. A lively breed that seldom regards its own size, or its frailty when in jeopardy, the Chihuahua proves to be a naturally hearty animal. After her first year, Sydne found very little to keep her down.

All in the Attitude

Laying a good foundation for, well, anything—is all about attitude. I hesitate to say that attitude makes or breaks, but I think it can be a final straw in many areas of life. A substantial part of my divorce recovery involved learning how to receive the merits of optimism. I learned that messages *(that's beyond me)* I may recite to myself *(I deserved that)* every day filter in negativity, often cleverly wrapped inside a train of other unrelated thoughts, just like in those two examples. Now Jim and I can readily recognize each other's negative train of thought, often before the engine leaves the station. We usually call each other down for a mental time-out.

Negativity is cyclic. If my view of the world is pessimistic, I will proceed with apprehension, expecting the worst. Since I've obviously visualized the worst, I'll most likely find it. Breaking cycles of negativity require mental war. I realized I had to be willing to first recognize my negative thinking, then counteract every single negative statement with a positive one. I sought to be thorough because I had learned: negativity kills.

Optimism, on the other hand, takes the elements I can change or control and focuses on achieving beneficial goals by initiating change. It's not realistic to be overly optimistic or pessimistic about forces beyond my control.

Optimism is extremely influential. I've seen good attitudes alter seemingly insurmountable circumstances. However we slice it, the overall effects of optimism are far more powerful and enriching to our relationship than all the rational deduction Jim and I can muster together on any given subject. The energy behind one ounce of optimism beats a ton of circumspection.

The foundation of our second marriage was an optimistic one. At the time, I was still learning about optimism. I'd begun to understand that negativity doesn't just creep out of the baseboards. Focus and attitude is just as practiced as anything else. Jim and I readily agree that so many aspects in life are touched first by how we think.

Resolving personal struggles after a divorce requires tons of optimism. Pairing two new households in a second marriage can introduce challenges that require even more reassurance than in the first. And one of the best ways to be reassuring is to be optimistic.

Early in our marriage, Jim began interjecting polite suggestions to change the subject away from fruitless discussions concerning the unchangeable features of our pasts.

"Let's not go there," he'd say.

On the surface, this might sound negative. But I soon began to see just how positive and valuable his deterrents were. Jim and I only reinforced negativity when we conversed about unchangeable circumstances, whether present or past. For those circumstances we solved nothing. We also realized that our conversations set a precedent for everything that followed. Ours is a precious friendship now, because we built it on smiles.

Optimism in Pints

I've noticed that optimism, for the most part, is delivered in small packages. What makes simple pleasures so special? "Oh, look honey—the baby just drooled the letter 'C' on your dinner jacket."

If optimism came in much larger packages, there's at least a handful of real cynics I know who'd be standing around asking, “What’s the catch?” Enthusiasm is far more believable in small doses. In fact, I’m not sure if anybody would accept windfall optimism for very long.

“Sorry, ma’am, I don’t care how many of your chickens can whistle the national anthem, we’ve already contracted Willie Nelson to sing the pregame show.”

We prefer reality, do we not? Optimism in pints, not kegs.

Nonetheless, I think we need some. In the aftermath of my divorce, I guess you could say I’d traded in everything for a Chihuahua. I prefer to think I was left holding three ounces of optimism.

Happy Contagions

A year later Sydne inherited Buck as a stepbrother and made it her business to pester him for the rest of his natural life. She complemented him in a therapy dog duo that touched many crippled and developmentally impaired children. I watched a little boy named Sydney perform his routine therapy exercises with extra gusto many times for the little dog with the same name as him. Sydne would sit on Sydney’s wheelchair tray for a treat and stir up volumes of energetic activity.

Sydne often bedded down with critically ill patients in hospitals and refused to budge. Like other accounts in which I’ve witnessed mysterious animal empathy at work, Sydne seemed to instinctively “know” the patients who needed the extra time and attention. If a dog treat became part of the picture, she was all the more interested, her long ears splayed and alert. The same hearty spirit that pushed her way past her own misery with a remarkable attitude has continued to win many smiles for years. But her greatest destiny was bridging a gap for me—from the painful emotional polarities following divorce to a greater understanding about optimism and attitude. She taught me that attitude shapes real love—which can believe, hope, and endure all things.

CHAPTER 4
Commitment

Though I met Oreo long before my first marriage, the truths about marital commitment were written all over that encounter. I can look back now and see how much was really there. Much like hidden pictures within a picture, how I committed myself to Oreo became a pattern for others—all the more clear with time, experience, and, possibly, the very best vantage point—hindsight.

Oreo

My best guess was, he'd simply wandered too far from home, a small Valée sheepdog barely distinguishable from the concrete median strip along North Central Expressway in Dallas. It was nearing the five o'clock rush hour. As I drove north in a steady funnel of workday commuters, I saw clearly that if this little dog left the median he didn't stand a chance.

I took the next exit to the U-turn access and looped back, praying that the little sheepdog would merely continue his fitful pacing along the median. Just north of him was an area broad enough for me to wedge my Datsun. My spontaneous plan was to backtrack on foot and somehow coax him to me.

North Central Expressway, or U.S. Highway 75, is no place to park a car. Out of curiosity, I later ran an accident report on the quarter-mile stretch where I parked my car that day. The highway department's records bureau reports nearly two hundred motor vehicle accidents annually on that quarter of a mile alone. I could've very easily caused an accident.

But I was committed to saving, if possible, this little sheepdog. I spotted him again, still trotting up and down the median as I drove around. He had the characteristic shaggy and motley coat of a sheepdog, his eyes completely hooded.

Not until I stepped out of my car with the sea of traffic whizzing past and walked into a smattering of taunting honks did I consider the possibility that this little sheepdog might not come to me. He seemed to be limping. Myriad possibilities raced through my thoughts: he might be rabid, or wary of strangers, or simply too frightened to respond to my calls. We might distract another motorist and cause an accident. Or even worse: I might drive him, in my attempt to help, back out into the highway.

He came forward as I approached him, a good sign. When I stooped and held out my hand, he continued to hobble his way toward me. My petting him earned the reward of a generous lick. He was wearing a collar with a tag engraved with the name "Oreo" and a telephone number.

The next challenge was getting Oreo to my car. Because of his injury, I didn't feel safe about picking him up. But I didn't want to risk his running out into traffic, either. He seemed happy enough to see me, verified by a constant wagging of his tail.

I very carefully sandwiched his torso between my arms, carrying him with the injured hip away from my body. He didn't seem to mind. I sat him in the passenger's seat, where he promptly flopped down.

His condition and reactions told me several details about Oreo: he was well cared for, accustomed to being handled, and simply taken with car rides. He hadn't sustained a life-threatening injury. As I drove on, I tried to reach his owners with my cell phone. The line was busy.

I could tell by the telephone number's prefix that Oreo didn't live too far from me, probably just on the other side of the expressway. After several tries the line was still busy, so I gave up on the possibility of a quick doggie delivery and took him home with me.

Oreo was glad to be off the highway. My home became his discovery zone for the next few minutes while I tried again to reach his owners. The line was still busy.

At that time, I was single and owned no pets. I rifled through the kitchen cabinets for a Tupperware bowl to give Oreo some water and searched for some food scraps. He ate a little, but seemed more interested in alternately discovering and resting.

The line was still busy. I began to fear the number had been changed or disconnected without an update to Oreo's tag. I began thinking about the possibility of inheriting a dog. But I wasn't going to give up that easily. Oreo wanted to go home.

With each decision about Oreo's safety and well-being, I'd stepped in deeper. At any given point, I realized, I could've turned away from my rescue efforts. I could've simply driven past him the first time I saw him. I could've stopped, then decided to leave well enough alone. I could've driven him to the neighborhood where I thought he belonged and dropped him off. But none of those possibilities completed the task of absolutely ensuring Oreo's likelihood of survival.

I decided to have the operator confirm this was a working number, interrupt the call, explain the emergency, and give the owner my number. With that done, I received a call a few minutes later from a very ecstatic mother.

As it turns out, Oreo had been missing about a day. The family had notified the *Dallas Morning News* and several radio stations. An anxious mother in gardening attire and her nine-year-old son were delighted to see their dog.

"Oreo!" The little boy and his dog met each other, air-bound, in my living room. Oreo dove into the boy's freckled arms and slathered him with licks.

Mom, tearful, was already fishing out her checkbook, explaining that somebody in a construction crew had left the gate to their backyard open yesterday.

"How do you think he got down into the expressway?" she asked.

I didn't have a good explanation. That section of North Central Expressway was barricaded on either side by twenty-foot embankments. Oreo had somehow navigated himself along a very dangerous stretch of highway. Perhaps a fall accounted for his injury.

I was glad to hear that the next stop for Oreo was the vet. They insisted, too, that I accept a reward.

But the greatest reward for me was finishing a commitment I'd started, a whole sequence of events fueled by emotion and logic that culminated with Oreo finding his way safely back home.

Keeping My Word

Commitment, by its very definition, is a proactive word—to do, or not to do. While its nature pulls me toward seeing a task through, I can wade deeper into any situation hinging on my determination to complete my pledge. I can pledge to keep my word. I can pledge to abstain from a personal vice. I can pledge to join a club or organization in keeping with its rules and standards.

Thus a commitment, which starts out as a pledge, carries with it the nuances of *not doing* as well as *doing*, as well as *setting out to do*. A pledge becomes only as good as the strength of my word, or my capacity to follow through.

A marriage commitment is a good example of a pledge with a capital "P" that begins by keeping my word about the little things. Commitment in the little things—in everyday life—requires discipline. If I bind myself to a day-in, day-out resolve to keep my word about anything I do, commitment becomes a natural outworking of my own personal integrity. Developing the resolve to keep one's word is, simply put, acquiring a good habit.

Many people I know have developed valuable personal assets from standing behind their word—dauntless perseverance, professional success, effective role modeling, and capable leadership. My husband, Jim, is a good example of a man driven by strong commitments. The demands of his profession as a physician require it. He shows me every day that being dedicated to the small things brings success where it counts. It's true that God is in the details.

When the issue of commitment comes up in the context of a divorce, it's easy to make an automatic assumption that all divorces occur in absence of commitment, or that the marriage dissolved because one or both partners had a problem committing. Nothing could be further from the truth.

Life involves layers of commitments every single day. Some obligations over time become routine, like driving my child to school. Nevertheless, even this obligation requires a certain level of personal responsibility and introduces degrees of risk (as in this example, the risk of an accident, the risk of arriving late, or the risk of receiving a traffic ticket). Other priorities, such as shopping for an out-of-print cookbook, while less important to me, may nonetheless require much more concerted effort. Or if that cookbook is needed for my child's school project, for example, the nature of that commitment changes again.

The sheer amount of decisions I garner within each twenty-four-hour period concerning myself, my spouse, and my child can be mind-boggling. Added to that, commitments and responsibilities often overlap. Clear-cut decisions don't always show themselves that easily. Jim has his personal decisions that often overlap mine, and soon our son will be making his own choices as well. The problem with committing to do anything is that no decision in life occurs in a vacuum; therefore, nothing can completely prepare me for all the ramifications of everything I do.

It's been my experience that most problems in a marriage occur not by failure to commit, but to what we commit ourselves. At one time or another I know I've engaged in activities mindlessly and heartlessly. I've taken small miracles and everyday blessings for granted. I understand what it means to go through the motions and ascribe to knee-jerk values without deeply questioning why.

In the end, commitment is only as important as the integrity of my word. If I choose to end one commitment and take up another, this doesn't necessarily mean I've forsaken my personal values or absolutes.

Absolutes simply set standards for living. Values can strengthen me in my commitments and guide me in discontinuing them as well. If I choose to end a commitment, my decision doesn't necessarily indicate an erosion of values.

Commitment for Chickens

I guess I've read one too many collections from the *Far Side* by Gary Larson, because when I think of the ultimate marriage commitment, I see two chickens standing in wedding attire in front of a Las Vegas chapel, the groom sweating bullets (literally). The chapel facade, of course, is merely a flat supported by sawhorses, and the building behind it is actually a poultry-processing plant. The "pews" are conveyor belts crowded with assembly-line workers cleaning chickens. The caption: *A Chicken's Problem With Commitment.*

Who knows what life may bring? My eyelids may fall off! I may never see the other side of the moon . . .

It's a tough job, but somebody's got to do it. Some of us get past the chapel part. Some don't. But if you've come this far, I'd say it's time to glue your eyelids on, keep in touch with your friends at NASA, tie the knot, and hang on!

A C-World

Losing a relationship is not about a failure to commit. It's about a failure to discriminate what is best for the relationship. It's about day-to-day decisions.

I would love to believe that in my attempt and commitment to rescue Oreo, the way that situation resolved was the only way in this world it could've resolved because of my fierce commitment. But the fact is, Oreo could've decided to take a dodge into the expressway before I was able to make my way back. Or he could've been frightened enough to run from me. Life doesn't occur in a vacuum.

I set out with determination, but my resolve doesn't guarantee control of any given situation. Commitment, as Oreo taught me, isn't about control.

If I remain aware that life doesn't always offer ideal circumstances for every choice and that I don't have total control, then I can realistically set out to follow my pledge. I cannot prevail over every repercussion in life. But for each Oreo who finds his way home, I will smile.

CHAPTER 5
Expectations

I'm no expert on reptiles, but for me, cold-blooded, water-bound pets don't cultivate any particular feelings of affection. My encounters with my own fish tanks and friends' iguanas never won me over—except for an unusual visit with a box turtle named Gladys. Aside from endearing me, Gladys startled me into a new reality. She was more than I'd ever dreamed a turtle could possibly be.

I was engaged, about to enter the wedding chapel a second time around, and I had to reckon with several concerns: What did I expect? What was expected of me? Would we disappoint each other, and what would we do about it?

Gladys

Gladys was hatched in a construction pit. Her owner plucked up this tiny baby turtle just before a front-end loader leveled the remains of the pile during the last leg of a home remodeling. Gladys, then about two inches long, found a new home inside an elaborate terrarium neatly landscaped with fern, pine bark, sand, and a wading pond. When I first met Gladys, she was still olive green, body and shell alike, with little white speckling on her neck that sparkled like snow.

Gladys's owner, Rachel, had quickly bonded with her, and I could see why. Gladys would strain her head far out of her shell to make contact with a pat from an index finger, then lean her neck into it, like a dog or cat snuggles into a good ear scratching. With a magnifying glass I could better see Gladys's eyes—not just your frigid and beady reptilian winkers—but arresting, black orbs that searched beyond my finger to my face.

Rachel, a well-tanned, earthy woman who runs an Internet employment service out of her home, became this turtle's personal playground outside of the terrarium. Gladys would paddle her way around the neckline of Rachel's sweater, sunbathe on her collarbone, and nest on her shoulder. The responsive and affectionate behavior of this tiny box turtle was fascinating to watch. Gladys surpassed all my expectations about turtles as companion pets, and about reptiles in general.

During a "happening" party at Rachel's one evening, I found Gladys sitting in the corner of her terrarium, her head and legs tightly retracted into her shell.

"You think the noise bothers her?" I asked.

Rachel smiled. "Nah, she's cool."

I picked up the magnifying glass and looked for signs of life. "Is she sick?"

Rachel came closer. "She's okay. She's just mad."

"How can you tell?"

Rachel nudged Gladys's shell with her finger, earning a swat from a hind leg. Back into the shell Gladys went, slammed tight.

Rachel just laughed. "I clean her terrarium every Friday," she explained. She scooped up a few rocks and transferred them to the other side of the wading pond. "I try to put things back the way she has them, but she always notices."

Recharting Expectations

Expectations are the stuff dreams are made of. While unrealistic expectations can be a setup for great disappointments, realistic expectations can become viable power sources for achieving goals and dreams. When expectations get out of balance, life can become a tightrope stretched between anticipation and letdown.

In a relationship, I come to a partnership with my own unique goals—realized and unrealized. I join my mate with his anticipations and struggles, which will converge and diverge with my own. I must keep in mind that much of what Jim and I expect in life was imprinted on us as children. Expectations involve a series of variables that include personality, constitution, background, and life experiences.

I've observed that some people dream big, others small. Some stifle their dreams in lieu of personal responsibility, while others gamble their dreams away. Some live in their dreams, and others in their disappointments.

In a good relationship, I'll evaluate how hard I can push for my goals with respect to sharing and supporting my partner's dreams. A healthy relationship integrates expectations and dreams—particularly the diverse. I don't think this necessarily mandates wives turning wrenches or husbands knitting one, purling two. It's simply a willingness to step outside of my own interests and acknowledge the importance of my partner's individuality, his expectations, his dreams.

The closer I come to accepting that I am not a carbon copy of Jim's must-bes, must-dos, must-haves, or must-nots, the closer we are to integrating our expectations in a peaceful, healthy manner. Jim and I do not view the world exactly the same way, and we don't expect ourselves to.

When personal differences occur, I like to do something I call "recharting expectations."

I put on the brakes, take a step back, and ask:

- "Where am I going with this?"
- "Why am I doing this?"
- "Is there another way?"

If I'm willing to rechart my goals and Jim is willing to be part of the process, we can move past our possibly misguided expectations with fonder and truer aspirations for our future. Since Jim and I both have the nagging habit of setting difficult goals for ourselves, we've recharted our expectations several times already. Though evaluating and changing our expectations is difficult, no doubt about it—the reward of unity and harmony is always worth the extra effort.

Going into a new relationship naturally offered me new expectations, while others remained the same. The second time around I was better equipped to handle disappointments and weather the risks of personal failure. Most of all, I had a partner who reciprocated my hopes and dreams with respect for my time, energies, and limitations.

Daring to dream and expecting the best to come after a devastating relationship loss can be quite an undertaking. But I think the risks involved are worth taking the plunge, especially when you're there to watch your new partner's dreams come true.

This Li'l Piggy

Now here's another thing about expectations—the story of the li'l piggies—which can cure a bad case of cabin fever for little tykes on long road trips like a charm. I yank off my son's shoes and socks, tug his toes, and make sure to squeal out loudly the wee-wee-wee on the all the way home. I've used it so frequently when the road-trip trolls come out to pester my son, I really don't have to pull his toes any more. Fingers do just as well, with a fraction of the work.

The payoff is the last little pig, of course. But my son is anticipating the squeal from the first grab of his toes—or fingers, if you will. His little grin grows broader with every verse, and those huge brown eyes gleam brighter with every tug. He usually starts giggling uncontrollably by the fourth pig.

A couple of times out of sheer mischief I've substituted *woof-woof, yee-haw,* or some other ridiculous tag in the place of the traditional wee-wee-wee at the end. His reaction is always the same. Nothing can put a lid on that kid's laughter, because the rhyme is so cleverly crafted to generate anticipation—expectations of the big finale, the loud squeal of the last little piggy.

So now when I think about great expectations, I think about li'l piggy payoffs. Works every time.

Expecting Reality

My experience with Gladys illustrates case-in-point how my expectations about her capabilities as a companion pet were largely misguided by my ignorance of, and limited experience with, reptiles. I met her with a certain bias about how she was supposed to appear and act. Although my actual experience with Gladys proved to be a pleasant versus disappointing one, it warned me about the Achilles heel of assuming too little as well as too much.

Jim and I have seen that so much of blending our expectations as partners lies in our willingness to admit that preconceived notions may very well mislead us, and that we can rise above even these to achieve together more realistic goals and satisfactory dreams.

CHAPTER 6
Good and Bad

Shortly before I began college, I fell in and out of first love, a summer blended with memorable hard knocks and a horse named Jubilee. Jubilee was a forerunner of much more good and bad to come—a summer of joy blended with sadness that would largely shape my destiny. He was the genesis, a new awareness about how I would execute living and loving in triumph and trouble.

JUBILEE

His official name—*Nantucket's Texas Jubilee*—came after much deliberation and elimination by the American Quarter Horse Association, which served me with a list of horses already registered under the names *Jubilee and Texas Jubilee.* My grandfather bought him on an auction block after bidding up the price twice and had purchased him before I knew what was happening.

Jubilee caught my eye the moment he entered the auction ring. He was only six months old, a nameless colt prancing and tossing around his platinum mane. He had a striking palomino coat that brushed out to a fine sheen. I could hardly wait until he was old enough to ride.

According to horse and cattle superstition, Jubilee had just about every mark of unpredictability. In short, he was guaranteed to be wild. He had one white forefoot, one black hoof, and a blaze that extended into his lip. He frequently showed the whites of his eyes. He was born on April Fools' Day.

As far as breaking went, Jubilee lived up to his reputation. The trainers who broke him were forced to saddle and mount him in a cattle chute. He rarely loaded in a trailer without a struggle after that.

Jubilee was a horse probably never meant to be ridden. But when I looked at Jubilee, I saw a beautiful animal. I was convinced that, with frequent riding and proper training, I could bring out the best in him. My formula wasn't inventive in the least. I would find power in routine and persistence. I would simply ride him two hours a day, six days a week.

Jubilee was the fourth horse I'd owned. Though experience was on my side, I was thrown from him more times than any other. My first attempt to saddle him left me with a substantial rope burn and sitting in a trail of dust, Jubilee bucking to the far end of the corral. After that jolly experience, the taming of Jubilee became my foremost ambition.

The first task was moving Jubilee from a larger stable and pasture to a half-acre pen behind my house. My father and I constructed the stables over one weekend. Now Jubilee's only source of food was oats at five, and his main exercise was the daily ride.

Jubilee responded amazingly well to routine and structure. By the end of the summer, I rode him bareback. He had an exemplary single-foot trot and a canter smooth enough to read by. He quickly learned to tack on command, both for riding and halter showing. But he needed riding daily to keep his energy reserves at a manageable level.

When I enrolled in college that fall, I knew the daily rides would soon end. I had a full course load with no spare time for the training Jubilee needed. I couldn't bear to see him lose what he'd gained. Jubilee had proved himself a remarkable horse with consistent riding. I was fortunate to find a buyer who understood Jubilee's temperament and promised to continue where I left off.

The Hard Knocks Prop

To me, Jubilee's story illustrates the ups and downs, or the good and bad, of horsemanship. Given over to the wrong hands, Jubilee would've been quickly on his way to the glue factory. He had enough craziness in his basic nature to overlook his show-quality looks and wonderful gait. Long hours went into calming him to the point I could enjoy his good qualities.

I'm not suggesting that good and bad are qualities I can instill into another human being. The dispensing of good and bad is obviously not always within my power to control.

In a less than ideal world, I will encounter good times and hard times that are external to my relationships with other people, as well as my own internal experiences of good and evil. Both forces—external and internal—shape my experience as an individual and a partner.

Jim and I agree that life is often a tug of war between good and bad, and that the places we choose to occupy along the rope can permanently alter our experience. Within traditional marriage vows Jim and I pledged for the second time to accept the bad with the good. I never bought into that part of the vow, however, to mean we are locked into accepting unnecessary hardship or embracing evil for the sake of fulfilling our vows. If I bring unnecessary hardship into our relationship by my own selfishness or indiscretion, I am doing nothing more than foolishly putting our unity to the test. To bear up under self-imposed good and evil is not fulfilling my marriage vows.

It's easy to rationalize away bad behavior in the name of accepting the bad with the good. It's also easy to prop up the word "commitment" at the disposal of all the other fundamentals that go into making a relationship essentially enjoyable. Being committed to weather adversity in a relationship doesn't give me a license to create hardship. Jim and I try to remain constantly aware of this principle as we share the daily ups and downs.

I think author C. S. Lewis said it best: " . . . whatever its merits, self-torture is quite a different thing from tribulation sent by God. Everyone knows that fasting is a different experience from missing your dinner by accident or through poverty."

When I contribute my best to our relationship and refuse to excuse my own misdeeds as affliction, the joy and sorrow I then share with Jim can contribute to our intimacy. We catch our breath in times of joy. I learn far more about myself, Jim, and the spirit of our relationship in times of adversity. Jim and I have noticed that the inevitable hard knocks, so often occurring at times when we least expect them, show us who we are, and, more important, who we can be.

Baby Questions

In terms of completely explaining good and bad, I think we come down to one of life's perplexing moments. The stuff we're made of, the rubber that meets the road, the cookie that crumbles. Just let a six-year-old question-box follow you around for a few hours, and you'll have good and bad all figured out. Maybe.

Kiddo: "Why do we have jails?"

You: "Because some people do bad things. We have to lock them up."

Kiddo: "Why?"

You: "To keep them from doing more bad things."

Kiddo: "Why?"

You: "Because the things they do hurt other people, like me and you."

Kiddo: "Why?"

You: "Different reasons. Some bad people might be born that way. Other bad people had bad things done to them, so they want to be mean to other people."

Kiddo: "Why?"

You: "Oh, I don't know. I guess because it makes them feel good."

At this point the inquiring six-year-old seems momentarily satisfied. Then: "But if bad people can feel good, how can they be bad?"

A Horse Trade

Without experiencing the bad, could I fully appreciate the good? Probably not.

If given the opportunity, would I have traded Jubilee's looks and gait for a better temperament? Possibly. But this is now and that was then. The reality is, I cannot experience one without the other, good or bad.

In the small town where I grew up, a horseback rider usually merited right of way, and as a teenager, I rode everywhere—farm roads and highways, the main drag, even into fast-food drive-thrus. Jubilee adapted to traffic, dogs, pedestrians, and many situations that would've otherwise spooked him before. Within his restless makeup, he proved many times over to me that he'd found the proper balance, or a way to use his hypersensitivity to help me out.

I've had a neurological hearing impairment since birth, and riding a horse in traffic or crowds can be tricky. Jubilee became my ears. His reactions in these situations were always predictable. He'd set his ears a certain way, or turn his head just so. I quickly learned to read his signals, about twenty in all. A quick turn of the head to the left with the ear slightly aft meant a fast approaching truck, rear left, for example.

Over the years I've eked out a personal philosophy—not yet proven in every circumstance—that all people living out their intrinsic experiences are torn between cultivating and overcoming their own personal demons. To trade places with someone else—to actually crawl into somebody else's skin for a single minute—would be my undoing. I am road-tested for my problems only. A combination of individual constitution and personality coupled with the school of life and some well-developed coping mechanisms garner each of us with the capacity to squirm through our own dire straits.

When it comes to pairing two lives and sharing the ups and downs, I must admit I'd find little joy or satisfaction in dodging pneumatic coughs or extracting ingrown toenails, some of the daily grind that brings my husband fulfillment with a job well done. On the other hand, he has more than once ranked this business of writing in league with the number-one neurotic profession of pole-vaulting. Thus, neither Jim nor I are cut out to walk exactly in each other's shoes, which yields us freedom to express that though we may not completely understand each other's innermost drives all the time, out of love we will take the opportunity to try.

For how I choose to attend my pain, share my happiness, and allow good and bad to draw me into a deeper intimacy with Jim is, at last, a remarkable privilege.

CHAPTER 7
Unity

Jasper, a baby raccoon, was a step away from the ordinary, a premonitory call to motherhood and a unity like I'd never imagined. Several years after meeting Jasper, I was fortunate enough to enter such a unity in my second marriage. Next to meeting each other, those two little lines Jim and I saw in the well of a QuickVue pregnancy test changed our lives above everything else. We were about to become parents.

Jasper

Jasper appeared on my porch with his mother in tow one evening at dusk. All I saw were four bright black eyes peering through the window.

I was familiar with the eating habits of these garbage-pail scavengers. I put out a tray of food scraps and a tub of water, knowing those raccoons would soon be back. This routine went on for several nights until the evening I fell off the clock and fed later than usual.

Barefoot, I stepped out onto the porch. Something rustled across my foot. I looked down to see Jasper and his mom circling me like a pair of hungry cats. Startled, I immediately set down the tray and edged my way back inside.

I watched those two for a few more nights as Jasper learned the ways and means of eating solids, negotiating trees, and dumping the water tub. Sometimes I would sit outside while they ate, beckoning his mom with a cookie. I didn't expect Jasper to catch on, but he did. He soon came up to take his turn. Not wanting to frighten him, I started to lay the cookie on the ground, but Jasper beat me to it. He scampered up, took the prize in his jaws, and placed one paw on my wrist to lever it out of my grip.

I've never forgotten the light, damp pressure of those tiny paw pads on my wrist. I've since observed that the most minute biological movements, especially those of babies—our own children—can captivate us above everything else.

Crowning a Unity

Throughout history—in civilizations high and low, from kingships to boweries—the cultural mandate to reproduce, whether random or ordered, has been viewed as unifying progeny, symbolizing prosperity, and ensuring the survival of the species. But taken to its grass roots, can producing children bring unity into a marriage?

Yes, and no.

An informal survey of friends, family, parents, and children who have been through divorce yielded the following helpful information:

Obviously, children don't prevent divorce. But in the presence of an existing healthy unity, children can help further solidify and even redirect the course of that relationship as Mom and Dad begin their roles as parents. The key is what's already happening to the partnership before children come along.

If intimacy with my partner has been built on a healthy attraction and a solid friendship that nurtures all the optimism, commitment, and spirituality two people can possibly share—then children enter the relationship as a complement, or a crown, to the relationship that already exists.

The added responsibilities of loving, directing, and disciplining a child casts a unique dimension to a person's individuality as he or she begins serving as a parent. Parenting, much like developing healthy intimacy, stretches us—to be physically and spiritually whole, to love unreservedly, and to ensure the fittest survival of our young.

Unfortunately, unity is not a prerequisite for children. The hard truth is that even in twenty-first-century Western civilization I can instinctively marry and procreate without much guidance, unity, or otherwise in my life.

An independent study of marriages conducted a few years ago documented that a large percentage of divorces occur around the four-year mark—enough time to rear a single child through infancy. This raises an interesting question: Does attraction and marriage serve only as an evolutionary drive to propagate, or ensure survival of the species?

On the one hand, this appears to be so, since children don't repair faltering relationships between adults at a very high success rate. To reassure children that this isn't their job, parents who divorce may be called to a double duty. While recovering from their own relationship loss, they must reinstate their love, support, and authority as newly single parents.

Stacking up the life changes during a divorce, recovery, and new, emerging unity, it's only natural and responsible to be concerned about the continued developmental needs of our children and how these changes affect them. A new relationship will transit more smoothly into a child's life if both natural parents, particularly the nonresidential one, clearly communicate their continued love, protection, and support. Children must understand that their parents are divorcing as husband and wife, not as mother and father.

On the other hand, children can learn from parents who will admit their own mistakes and make visible efforts to change and grow. Though children may have difficulty fully accepting a new significant other or stepparent, if the new relationship is a healthy one, they will have a better model for unity over the long term than from the original marriage. Each divorce, with its own unique features, still faces the general dynamics and challenges of introducing a child into a new household—challenges that involve the child's understanding of who's in charge, who will listen, and who will be there.

Children are living beings embarking on the rest of their lives. We owe it to them. We owe it to ourselves.

The State of the Union

Now, I suppose, in terms of keeping tabs on how our relationships are going, we could do a lot worse than creating a few extra mouths to feed. Imagine if, in every instance of marital discord, we received a letter straight from the federal government. Yep, every time we'd load the dishwasher . . .

To Whom it May Concern:

In a great marital crisis such as yours, unanimity of action among those seeking a common end (i.e., your dishwasher happily loaded) is very desirable. Yet no approach to such unanimity is attainable unless some deference (drinks on you) be paid to the will of the majority (your in-laws).

In this case (loading your dishwasher), the common end appears to be the maintenance of the Union, and among the means (e.g., lots of promises) to secure that end, such will, through an election (drawing straws), be most clearly declared in favor of a constitutional amendment (adding at least one dependent to your household for tax purposes).

The most reliable indication of public purpose in this matter is derived through popular elections (your friends drawing straws). Judging by the recent canvass and its result, the purpose of the people within the loyal States (your true friends) to maintain the integrity of the Union was never more firm than now. The extraordinary calmness and good order with which they mingled at the polls (knocked back shots at the local bar) give strong reassurance of this. There has nonetheless been much heated controversy as to the proper means of advancing the Union cause (the appropriate way to load shot glasses into your dishwasher).

The manner of continuing the effort (to load your dishwasher) remains to choose. On careful consideration of all the evidence accessible (dirty dishes), it seems to us that no attempt at negotiation with the insurgent leader (okay, it's one of you) could result in any good. The issue is distinct, simple, and inflexible.

You can at any moment have peace simply by laying down your arms and submitting to the national authority under the Constitution (running for Congress or joining the Peace Corps). If questions should remain, we will adjust them by the peaceful means of legislation. (All remissions of forfeitures should be postmarked correctly and mailed directly to the IRS.)

If the people (your friends) should, by whatever mode or means, make it an executive decision to reenslave such persons (you two), we will revoke all knowledge of this letter. We mean simply to say that the war (over your dishwasher) will cease on the part of the government (these letters) whenever it shall have ceased on the part of those who started it.

Whew.

A New Beginning

The masked duo disappeared off my porch and out of my life just as suddenly as they'd come. I left food out for another week before giving up. I kept reminding myself that, after all, these raccoons were scavengers. Nothing personal. They'd found better cooking somewhere else.

The neighbors across the farm road from me, in fact, were the new feeding trough. Mrs. Ella Montgomery, a slight woman who goes to the mailbox in her bonnet and bakes a mean pecan pie, had attracted the pair with appetizing aromas wafting from her kitchen. Ella and her husband, Frank, were keeping their seven-year-old great-grandson, Jacob, for the summer. Turns out that Jacob's father was regrouping after an extensive separation and divorce. Both parents agreed that Jacob, too, needed a break. So he was visiting his paternal great-grandparents and talking to the raccoons at night.

Frank, a cautious and doting man with a long face, would allow Jacob to put food out and watch from the window in his bedroom. On the second or third night running, he overheard Jacob talking to the raccoons. Ella finally worked up the nerve to interrupt. She walked into Jacob's room one night and sat on the windowsill with Jacob.

"What are they saying, Jacob?"

"The baby says he doesn't bite. And they want me to come outside and play."

Ella smiled, but not too much. "That so?"

Jacob nodded. "The baby has a daddy. But his daddy's always working too."

"I see." Ella listened to Jacob talk to the raccoons for a minute. He had his mom's bright, expressive eyes and his dad's slow, inquiring temperament. He was tall for his age and was rapidly outgrowing all his clothes.

"He misses his daddy sometimes," Jacob said. "His parents are divorced too."

Ella wasn't sure what to say. "Does his daddy live nearby where they can visit?"

Jacob nodded. "But sometimes the baby doesn't miss his daddy that much. He says he'd rather be by himself."

Ella forged ahead. "When the baby's with his daddy, does the baby miss his mommy?"

Jacob shrugged. “A little. She’s always tired and grumpy.”

Ella bit her lip and waited for Jacob to say something more. When he didn’t, she asked, “Is your friend, raccoon, sad?”

Jacob thought a minute. “He says it’s like having a cold in the summer when there’s no school to miss.”

“That’s no fun.”

“No, it’s not.” Jacob listened again. “He wants to know what he should do.”

Ella thought she understood what Jacob was asking. “Tell your friend, raccoon, if he feels sad, or mad, or confused, he doesn’t have to pretend it doesn’t matter, or think that he deserves to feel that way. He must realize that no matter what, his mommy and daddy still love him very much. And his great-grandma and grandpa, they love him more than anything in this world.” Ella poured everything out before she remembered that Jacob hadn’t told her anything about the raccoon’s “grandparents,” let alone great-grandparents.

Jacob turned to Ella with a huge smile. “I knew it.”

Ella inwardly cringed. He’d found her out. “What?” Though trying not to sound flustered, her voice went up a notch.

“You’ve been talking to the raccoons too!”

Jasper came to me again, years later. But this Jasper who came into my new unity was the child I carried and brought into this world. If not for him, Jim and I would've never known such healing. Healing had taken place in our lives, but not of the same medicine as holding our child's hand. Children can transport our hearts to places where yesterday's sorrows don't reach. Our Jasper emerged into our lives with such clarity and certainty, a tiny hand busy with securing life's delights and making our hearts sing.

CHAPTER 8 Beyond

Chipper reminds me about life's continuum as I move away from life before to life beyond. A North American fox squirrel, he was one of several my grandfather tamed in the latter years of his life.

I still make mistakes. I still fail to stop now and then to smell the roses. Sometimes I see the glass as half empty. But in all this, I learn. And I hope I'm still learning how to better smell a rose and look at water in a glass until the very end.

CHIPPER

My grandfather had a truly special way with wild creatures, and a ton of patience. He'd sit for hours in a lawn chair shelling pecans, tempting his backyard residents with their own form of fast food.

Over a period of several weeks, one squirrel came closer and closer. Soon my grandfather no longer had to toss the pecans so far away. Breakthrough day followed soon after: A squirrel he'd since named Chipper scampered up and sat on his foot.

Chipper, unlike some of the others, went beyond his backyard taming ground to bigger and better things. I'm not sure about the particulars, but I suspect that Chipper had watched my grandfather's daily routine for a very long time. So, when the old man cranked his van one morning to run his usual errands, Chipper was there. Waiting.

By that time, Chipper was also comfortable navigating shoulder to shoulder on his human companion, occasionally pausing to check out an earlobe or the topside view from my grandfather's head—and that's how he went for his first car ride.

Before long Chipper was the talk of the town. He made all the coffee breaks at the local gun dealer's, the feed store, and the automotive shop. My grandfather later informed us that Chipper took his coffee with cream. I can still see my grandfather's van pulling into the driveway with a squirrel hopping across the dashboard. With my grandfather as his chaperon, Chipper was fearless.

Every evening Chipper would return to his squirrel's life in the backyard. In the morning he would rejoin my grandfather for his fast life in the streets, amazing the local retirees and town merchants alike.

Chipper was also the star of my second-grade show-and-tell. My grandfather, dressed in his favorite beige coveralls, brought Chipper, riding on his shoulder. Suddenly, I was the kid in the classroom with the "cool" grandfather and his pet.

I couldn't understand, though, why my grandfather didn't keep such an extraordinary animal under lock and key. I feared for Chipper's safety in the greater outdoors.

"Don't you think he needs a warm bed?" I'd ask.

My grandfather would point to the big oak tree in his backyard. "He's got the best bed in the world, right up there."

Later, my grandfather's reasoning became obvious: Chipper was the phenomenon in our world because he maintained a connection with his own. His experience with humans was one that offered him only kindness and respect. Anyone could see that because Chipper felt safe enough under my grandfather's supervision, he was free to become the cute, daring, and trusting coffee companion he was. Chipper was also free to be wild, and my grandfather always handled him with a generous respect for his innate and peculiar awareness of danger.

The locals unanimously agreed that Chipper was a squirrel of somewhat exceptional intelligence. In public, he fascinated children and grownups alike as he meticulously cleaned his whiskers and leapt boldly onto outstretched arms. His sparkling black eyes housed an alertness—but more than that, a recognition—and an incredible awareness—about our humanness.

My grandfather set the precedent for the squirrel that came to coffee: he did not bring Chipper, he insisted; rather, Chipper brought himself. On a few rare days—perhaps according to some idiosyncratic and nameless squirrel almanac—Chipper apparently chose to miss his ride and remain in his own world. At times I still wonder if Chipper had any awareness about what rare and incredible moments he brought into ours.

Tapestry in Progress

Somewhere along the process of my recovery and discovery of new intimacy with Jim, I began truly seeing life as a continuum. I realized that if I am to master living in the present, I can't annihilate my past or refuse to plan for my future. I saw that, by and large, I live in a push-pull existence, with my past pulling me closer to my roots, and the present pushing me out—beyond.

Perhaps it's easier to think of this continuum like Chipper's worlds: I simply cannot exist in one without the other. What makes Jim or me function brilliantly or inefficiently in one is a carryover from the other. The future looks bright because the present feels good. Alternatively, the present may achieve nothing more for me if I ride in on the coattails of the same errors of the past.

If my personal time line represents a lifetime, I can fundamentally say that I carry my lifetime with me every waking moment. I am stretched between before and beyond, with a tenterhook buried in my past and a periscope nosing out into my future. I am layering choice upon choice, with hindsight as my teacher, the future as my pearl, and the present, a place where I sort through what I need to take from my past.

If my life is a tapestry in progress, and I could unravel away old threads of pain and disappointment from the underside (or annihilate certain events in my past), would I retain the same weave on the topside? Would extracting all the negative experiences remove the pattern quality I have gained on the topside, such as being more accountable or less presumptuous? Or, in my attempt to fill in these old gaps with newer thread (reweave my destiny without my past), would incongruities glare at us?

If, in my tapestry, a single running thread dating back to the oldest yarn continues to weave its way through, I will expect that it, too, will eventually appear faded and inconsistent next to the newer and brighter threads. As I scroll back through this tapestry, I see that the yarn at the beginning is the most faded, like that of the single running thread. If a single old thread treks its way through my personal history, it cannot change its constitution to match the present colors. Moreover, I would not want it to, for it represents my past. It is a grounding yarn, the part of me that forms an anchor in my continuum.

On the underbelly of this tapestry is life as it happens: a disorganized tumble of threads zigging around in all directions. The pattern on the opposite is how I develop: a combination of changing and unchanging parts of my personality and ability woven in by how I respond to life. Perhaps the pattern on the topside becomes more highly refined and ornate as I grow. Maybe it evolves into something that appears more skillful. Maybe it loses its creativity altogether.

When Jim and I look at the unpleasant events in our past as part of our individual tapestries, it helps us to embrace our divorces as indispensable parts of the mastery. On the one hand, our experiences might be best forgotten. But at second glance, I see a pattern on the topside emerging. And it is every bit as much a part of who I am, and who I will be.

A Farewell

Eight years after Chipper's first car ride, my grandfather stepped outside, dodging the first snap of winter on his way to retrieve the morning paper, and saw Chipper dead on the back stoop. They'd taken their coffee break together as usual the day before. But as the years had rolled past, we clearly saw that Chipper's days were numbered. He had succumbed to age like the rest of us. The hairs on his head and tail were hoary and thin, his movements calculated and slow. He no longer skirted the dashboard, but settled to ride quietly in the passenger's seat.

My grandfather found him still warm. Chipper had apparently passed the night in his squirrels' company, then had come to bid goodbye to an old friend who'd shown him another world.

Epilogue

As books go, I'd prefer that I never felt compelled to write this book. I'd prefer that no matter what comes or what is, with the right focus, enough faith, or exceptional work, you or I can mend any faltering relationship and restore its unity. But I would not be telling you the truth as I know it.

My ultimate goal in writing this book was to share with you, the reader, a journey—to find and maintain a healthy and spiritually satisfying life. In your journey, whether you choose to remain single, marry, divorce, or remarry becomes merely part of the superstructure. You.

In Part I, I made the formidable, painstaking, and at times facetious emotional path through a divorce recovery and eleven stages of grieving that relationship loss. In Part II, I entered a new marriage after divorce—a very different process from first love and marriage—and therein, eight stages leading to that intimacy.

Perhaps this book has challenged you to think in new ways. I hope it has motivated you to examine reality and what you hold true and dear in life. But most of all, I wish you wisdom.